BUILDING UTOPIA

BUILDING UTOPIA

ERECTING RUSSIA'S FIRST MODERN CITY, 1930

RICHARD CARTWRIGHT AUSTIN

THE KENT STATE UNIVERSITY PRESS   KENT & LONDON

ALL RIGHTS RESERVED

Library of Congress Catalog Card Number 2001007826
ISBN 0-87338-730-9
Manufactured in the United States of America

08   07   06   05   04   5   4   3   2   1

The Russian-language edition is translated by Galina N. Moleva and edited by Natalia Kolesnikova, published serially in the *Nizhny Novgorod Worker* (2001–2002).

LIBRARY OF CONGRESS CATALOGING-IN-PUBLICATION DATA

Austin, Richard Cartwright, 1934–
    Building utopia : erecting Russia's first modern city, 1930 / Richard Cartwright Austin.
        p. cm.
Includes bibliographical references and index.
    ISBN 0-87338-730-9 (alk. paper)
1. Automobile industry and trade—Russia (Federation)—Nizhniæi Novgorod—History. 2. Gor§kovskiæi avtomobil§nyæi zavod—History. 3. Ford Motor Company—History. 4. Austin Company—History. 5. City planning—Russia (Federation)—Nizhniæi Novgorod. 6. Nizhniæi Novgorod (Russia)—History. I. Title.
    HD9710.R93 N593 2003
    947'.41—dc21

2001007826

British Library Cataloging-in-Publication data are available.

FOR COLETTE

You held us together

CONTENTS

PREFACE

Early in 1998 Colette Mylott, personal secretary to my father for thirty-five years until his death, unlocked a desk drawer and handed me a leather ring binder containing letters that he had written from Russia in 1930 and 1931. Allan Austin was the youngest of twenty American engineers who assisted the Soviets in erecting Europe's largest automobile factory, as well as the first new city in Russia since the revolution—a city designed to express the social ideals of communism. Only Colette knew that these letters had survived.

The letters were written to Allan's father, Wilbert J. Austin, president of the Austin Company and at that time America's most innovative industrial builder. Wilbert, a confirmed capitalist and a devout Methodist, had contracted with the Soviet government to design these huge facilities and to supervise their erection on a remote site near the Volga River; to train peasants and young workers in modern construction techniques; and to complete the entire task in two years. It was the most ambitious development project yet undertaken by the Soviet Union, the most challenging construction project ever attempted by the Austin Company, and quite probably the most remarkable project in the history of industrial construction to that time. The letters from a young engineer to his father tell the personal side of the story and offer striking insights into a revolutionary society. They bring this page of history to life.

While I had heard these stories myself from my parents, I now resolved to see the sites for myself. Heidi McCormack, a lifelong friend and chief operating officer for General Motors in Moscow, invited me to Russia. She made contacts with the Gorky Automobile Factory (GAZ), as the enterprise is now known. (Gorky, the city that became the hub of Soviet industry, has now reclaimed its original name, Nizhny Novgorod.) When my wife and I arrived there in July 1998, we were taken in hand by Natalia Kolesnikova, director of the GAZ Museum of History, and Galina Moleva of the GAZ Foreign Trade Firm. Now a private stock company, GAZ was eager to recover the story of its origins and of its links with the West. We shared all that we knew. The apartment buildings erected under my father's supervision were still standing and in use, and some of the original construction remained in the vast automotive complex.

At the end of our week together, I offered to search for an American museum that might join with the GAZ Museum to mount an exhibition depicting this unique history. My inquiries led me to the Crawford Auto-Aviation Museum at the Western Reserve Historical Society in Cleveland, Ohio, where the principal offices of the Austin Company are located. John Grabowski, director of research, was immediately taken with Allan Austin's letters. Edward Pershey told me that the Historical Society would soon erect a new Crawford Museum of Transportation and Industry, for which my proposal would be a natural venue.

Soon the museums were discussing plans for a sophisticated traveling exhibition to begin at the new Crawford Museum, visit other museums in America and in Russia, and find a permanent home at the GAZ Museum in Nizhny Novgorod. The Austin Company, ownership of which had been recently acquired by its management, was also eager to recover its history. The company loaned Heidi Makela to assist in this exhibition planning. As Makela searched company archives in Cleveland and Kolesnikova dug more deeply into museum and company archives in Russia, they uncovered important documents, artifacts, photographs, and motion pictures.

In September 1999 I returned to Nizhny Novgorod with a delegation from the Crawford Museum and began face-to-face planning with the GAZ Museum. During that week the Nizhny Novgorod Regional Archives were opened to our research. They contain important documents that had been held in secrecy.

On the final evening of our visit, Natalia Kolesnikova, Galina Moleva, and I agreed to attempt an additional project. I would prepare a manuscript on the construction effort in 1930 and 1931, based on my father's letters. Galina Moleva

№ 179 / 14303 Пятница, 24 сентября 1999

НОВОСТИ ДНЯ
хроника, факты, комментарии

Игорь ПОНЯЕВ

СОТРУДНИЧЕСТВО

За океаном объявился родственник

Американцы для своего музея готовы купить не только старые «эмки», но и новые «ГАЗели».

— Я должник ГАЗа. Не было бы завода, наверное, не было бы и меня, — подчеркнул Ричард Остин, чьи предки проектировали и строили Горьковский автогигант.

Возможно, американец слегка утрирует, но во времена великой депрессии в США контракт, заключенный на проектирование нашего завода, спас фирму «Остин» и ее руководителей от краха и непредсказуемых последствий.

Возможно, поэтому Ричард Остин полюбил и город, и ГАЗ. В прошлом году он уже приезжал к нам, а в начале нынешнего пришел в Западное резервное историческое общество США и рассказал о том, как кливлендские рабочие и специалисты участвовали в сооружении Горьковского автозавода. Это вызвало интерес, и американцы начали «откапывать» документы, архивы, фотографии. Как раз в это время в Кливленде открывался музей транспорта и промышленности, и идея сотрудничества двух стран в сфере автомобилестроения показалась свежей.

Вчера солидная американская делегация во главе с доктором философии

● Фото Романа ЯРОВИЦЫНА.

Эту экспозицию создадут к 2003 году. А в 2006 году планируется передвижную выставку показать в Москве и Нижнем

вали в Павлове, где встречались с коллекционерами-автолюбителями. Но на вопрос, за сколько кливлендцы могли

Richard Austin greets Fyodor Chinchenko, who as a young man worked on Worker's City construction and then continued in the automobile factory for his working life. *Nizhny Novgorod Worker*, 1998. *GAZ Museum of History*

xi

would translate the manuscript into Russian. Natalia Kolesnikova would edit it for a Russian audience. We would seek publication in both countries.

All documents used in the preparation of this narrative—originals where possible, copies where necessary—have been deposited at the Western Reserve Historical Society.

In addition to those mentioned earlier, two people deserve particular thanks. When Allan Austin became president of the Austin Company, Marvin Epstein assisted him with public relations and became the unofficial company historian. His reflections on my father and on the company have been invaluable.

I thank the editors at the Kent State University Press for their patient attention to this manuscript, and particularly Christine Brooks for her imaginative book design.

Anne Leibig, my wife, is the first reader of all that I write. Her thoughtful suggestions and her dependable support add to my joy in writing.

Dick Austin
Dungannon, Virginia
November, 2003

BUILDING UTOPIA

1

THE AUSTIN METHOD

In 1930 my father, Allan S. Austin, was the youngest of the American engineers who guided the construction of the first new city in the Soviet Union, a project that also required building the largest automobile factory in Europe. His letters home provide the day-by-day narrative at the heart of the remarkable story told here. My mother, Margretta Stroup Austin, was younger still when she accompanied him—she was twenty-two. Allan passed his twenty-fifth birthday on the trip to Russia. (I would be born several years later.) Despite their youth, these two embodied the skills and the values that this team of Americans brought to their work with the Russians.

My grandmother, Emma Stroup (pronounced Str*owp*), loved to tell the story of Allan and Margretta's "first date." It was the summer of 1919 when Allan was fourteen, Margretta not yet twelve. Allan arrived on a Saturday afternoon to take Margretta to a moving picture show. He drove his father's huge Packard Twin-Six (twelve cylinder) automobile. He was not a tall boy. From the window, my grandmother watched Allan escort Margretta to the high car, open the passenger door, and assist her up into the seat. Then he went round to the driver's

Margretta took this snapshot of Allan Austin on their honeymoon, just eight months before they embarked on another ocean voyage, to Russia. *Margretta Austin Jamieson Album*

side. After he seated himself, Allan could barely see out the windshield. Emma would release a fond, soft laugh as she brought this scene to mind. "Babes in the woods!" she would exclaim, and then again, softly to herself, "Babes in the woods."

The Austin and the Stroup families had met at the Windermere Methodist Church in East Cleveland, Ohio, and they became close friends as they worshipped together year after year. There were quite a few Methodists in the team that went to Russia in 1930. Methodism is an English Protestant church, founded in the eighteenth century in response to the hardships of the early industrial revolution. The Methodist movement appealed to dislocated families—those forced from their farms into England's coal mines, iron furnaces, and cotton mills, as well as those who left England for America. The early Methodists believed that people came to God through a "heartwarming experience" of personal discovery. To assist this process Methodists held emotional "revival meetings" in churches or even in the open air. Ministers organized those who responded into groups for mutual support and discipline—this was the "method" that gave the church its name. Methodists became thrifty, hardworking, and sober—alcohol, tobacco, and gambling were forbidden to them. These habits helped Methodist working families to prosper, so by the nineteenth century their children became the backbone of the English middle class, and also the American.

Margretta's father, Ner Stroup, was the minister who led the Windermere Methodist Church, while her mother, Emma Cartwright Stroup, was the evangelist, whose preaching helped to draw new people to the congregation. Emma's father, Elijah Cartwright, had been an ironworker. He emigrated from England to America in 1845 and worked thirty years tending blast furnaces—twelve hours a day, seven days a week. As Elijah treated the wounds of ironworkers during frequent strikes, he became famous for his healing touch. He also assisted with childbirth, delivering all of his own children and many others in the poor neighborhood. When new steel technology closed the iron mills, Elijah became a shopkeeper and a Methodist preacher.

His daughter Emma was not only a Methodist evangelist but also a leader in the struggle to secure for women the right to vote. She was a Christian socialist. Inspired by the New Testament, not by Karl Marx, she believed that government must represent the needs of common people and not favor the rich.

When my mother Margretta was six years old, she was riding in an automobile with her parents and her two older brothers when their auto was struck by a trolley car. As the auto was hurled down the track the three children were thrown free, but when it burst into flames the parents were trapped. Ner died from his burns, and Emma lost her left leg. For the remainder of her ninety-five years Emma walked with crutches. Nevertheless, she raised three fine children: a poet, another Methodist minister, and my mother.

Borrowing, perhaps unconsciously, from a Christian symbol for Christ—the alpha and the omega, "the beginning and the end"—Wilbert Austin designed in 1907 this symbol for his "Austin method." The method and the symbol are still in use a century later. *The Austin Company Archives*

The Austin heritage had its own drama. My great grandfather Samuel Austin learned the carpenter trade in England and then, in 1872, emigrated to Cleveland, Ohio, to find work. In 1881 he started his own construction company. Samuel was so skillful and honest that he never lacked for work. Samuel was also a strict Methodist. When the ridgepole was erected on one of his early buildings, the carpenters tied a small fir tree on top as a signal that they were ready for the customary reward of a bucket of beer. Samuel saw the signal, but instead of beer he would bring them a more expensive gift, a basket of oranges. His workers soon learned that Austin employees did not drink alcohol on the job. This standard, and many more of Samuel's principles, survived in the Austin Company for nearly a century. During his early years Samuel Austin built houses and stores. In the 1890s, he built some of Cleveland's first factories as well.

Samuel's only son, Wilbert J. Austin, as a child watched the family business grow. Wilbert secured a degree in mechanical engineering from the Case School of Applied Science in Cleveland, and then he studied architecture in Europe. After Wilbert joined his father's business in 1900, he developed a management strategy that would revolutionize the industrial construction industry in the United States. Relying upon the reputation for integrity that his father had earned, Wilbert offered to clients a single contract, which would include design of a building, all construction, and the installation of machinery and equipment. He called this "the Austin Method of undivided responsibility." Those willing to trust the Austin Company for an entire project would receive a better building in a shorter period of time, at a reasonable price agreed to in advance.

Thomas Edison's new electric-light industry was the first to respond. Between 1908 and 1913 the Austin Company built lightbulb factories all over the United States to meet the rising demand for electric lamps. Then Wilbert Austin designed the first wide-span steel trusses, which allowed modern assembly lines to be set up in factories with no pillars in the way. With the approach of the First World War, many industries hired Austin to build factories and railroad facilities, as well as the first airplane assembly plants, hangars, and airports. As projects spread across the United States, Wilbert Austin innovated again. He willingly negotiated labor contracts with the unions representing workers in the various construction trades. Workers were assured good wages

and working conditions; the Austin Company was assured a quality workforce wherever it needed to build.

In the 1920s the Austin Company became America's best known construction firm. In 1927, in Michigan, the Austin Company built the world's largest automobile factory to manufacture the "Pontiac Six" for the General Motors

Corporation. The Austin Method worked so well that this huge factory was completed in just seven months.

Russian specialists were among those who took note of this remarkable achievement. They had come to America to learn how the Soviet Union might acquire the technology to manufacture cars and trucks for itself.

That same year, Allan Austin graduated from Yale University with a degree that combined architecture, engineering, and building management. His ambition was to follow in the footsteps of his father and his grandfather. A few months later Margretta Stroup graduated from Stanford University in California—its youngest graduate up to that time—with a degree in English literature. Since Allan also had an ambition to court Margretta, Wilbert Austin assigned his son to construction projects in California. The couple announced their engagement on Margretta's twenty-first birthday, and they married the following summer, on July 17, 1929. Eight months later they were on their way to Russia.

2

"THOSE RUSSIANS ARE STARTING FRESH"

Henry Ford (1863–1947) was an industrial genius. He was also a man of many contradictions, but people idolized him in the 1920s. He had perfected the automobile assembly line, and in 1908 he had inaugurated the age of mass production with the "Model T" Ford. Then, in 1915, Ford raised wages for assembly-line workers to an unprecedented five dollars a day and gave them a profit-sharing plan in addition. He did this, he said, so workers could afford to own the car they manufactured—a worker could buy a $440 Model T with eighteen weeks' wages. The wage hike was a brilliant step, but it was also necessary in a full-employment economy. On the assembly line the repetitive tasks were so arduous that employees had been leaving whenever they could find other jobs. By raising wages Ford secured the stable workforce necessary for fast-moving, tedious work in an environment of ear-splitting noise. Later, at the onset of the Great Depression, when workers lacked alternatives, Ford cut wages.

At Henry Ford's Highland Park plant, ca. 1914, autoworkers on the Model T assembly line join the engine to the frame (*above*) and drop the body (*below*).
Henry Ford Museum & Greenfield Village

A Ford Model A sedan. *Western Reserve Historical Society*

Ford was a political isolationist but a business internationalist. In 1915, in an effort to end the First World War before the United States was drawn into it, Ford headed a privately sponsored peace expedition to Europe. Vladimir Lenin (1870–1924), then a Russian exile in Switzerland, applauded Ford's effort, for Lenin was trying to organize industrial workers across Europe to rise up against the war and its capitalist sponsors. Neither Ford's scheme nor Lenin's proved successful.

After the war Ford's "Fordson" tractors were shipped to the new Soviet Union by Herbert Hoover, director of American efforts to relieve famine in Europe. Lenin's government was so impressed that it purchased twenty-five thousand tractors from the Ford Motor Company during the next six years. The high wages that this company paid were intended to forestall union organizing, and Ford routinely purged organizers and communist sympathizers from its plants. These firings motivated a trickle of skilled Ford workers to emigrate to the Soviet Union. Russian engineers, assisted by these workers, replicated Fordson tractors piece by piece, and by 1926 they were producing "knock-off" tractors on a simple assembly line. The quality was poor, however, so in that same year the Soviets invited Ford to build a tractor factory in Russia. Ford executives, wary of Soviet labor practices and suspicious that a communist government might decide to expropriate such an important private business, declined.

Late in 1927, Henry Ford replaced the Model T with his new "Model A." The next summer Russian officials brought a new proposition to Detroit, "that the [Moscow Automobile] Trust should build a factory to make Ford units, at first using parts shipped from Detroit, but gradually shifting to Russian components. The Ford Company should consent to reproduction of its models, furnish blueprints, install machinery, and provide technical and mechanical assistance."[1] Ford rejected this initial Soviet proposal as too small to bother with.

Energy for a much more ambitious proposal came from N. Osinskii, head of the Central Statistical Administration in Moscow. Osinskii had participated in the talks with the Ford Motor Company. Upon his return Osinskii prepared a series of articles in which he argued that Russian automotive transport was "catastrophically backward" and that proposals like those made to Ford were "mere handicraft." He advocated construction of an automobile plant capable of producing at least a hundred thousand vehicles annually. Kurt Schultz, in a brilliant analysis of the Soviet bureaucratic conflicts surrounding the eventual construction of just such a factory, reports that more conservative critics within the Soviet government objected that Russia lacked the necessary infrastructure, such as good roads and repair facilities, and mechanical expertise to utilize so many vehicles. Osinskii responded that in Russia these could grow along with automobile production, just as they had in the United States. Such a factory might also be used in wartime for the production of tanks and military vehicles. Without it the Soviet Union would remain vulnerable: if the Red Army had to use "the Russian peasant cart against the American or European automobile," it would be "threatened with the heaviest losses, not to say defeats."[2]

Joseph Stalin, determined to advance industrialization swiftly despite any obstacles in his path, embraced Osinskii's proposal in his first Five Year Plan, announced on October 1, 1928. Osinskii joined a delegation from "Autostroy" (an acronym for "State Bureau for Building of the Automobile Plant," as the Russian effort was now called) that promptly returned to Ford with an offer to cooperate on the largest automobile factory in Europe. It would be built east of Moscow near Nizhny Novgorod, an ancient Volga River trading city surrounded by a densely populated agricultural region from which unskilled labor might be secured.

Documents recently discovered in the Nizhny Novgorod regional archives reveal that in the spring of 1929, when negotiations with Ford threatened to break down, the Soviets explored with an American engineer the possibility

After signing the contract, Henry Ford (*center*) posed with two Soviet officials, Valery I. Mezhlauk, vice chairman of the Supreme Council of the National Economy of the USSR, and Saul G. Bron, president of the Amtorg Trading Corporation. *GAZ Museum of History*

of "pirating" Model A designs and manufacturing equipment to construct their own assembly line. The Soviets also put out feelers to the General Motors Company and staged a conspicuous debate in Moscow over the relative merits of the four-cylinder Ford Model A and GM's six-cylinder Chevrolet. Henry Ford could not restrain himself. He countered with an offer to supply the Ford V-8, then on the drawing boards.

A Ford Model AA pickup truck, 1929 model. *Western Reserve Historical Society*

The Soviets, however, knew exactly which vehicles they wanted. On May 31, 1929, the Supreme Council of National Economy of the USSR (VSNH) signed a thirty-million-dollar contract with the Ford Motor Company to equip a huge factory for the production of Model A cars, "Model AA" pickup trucks, and some heavier trucks. The factory would have the capacity to produce a hundred thousand vehicles a year—about thirty thousand cars and seventy thousand trucks. Soviet workers would assemble seventy-four thousand Ford cars and trucks from American parts, while Ford technicians trained them in the operation of their own manufacturing and assembly facilities.

This was a splendid deal for both sides. The Model A was the simplest design and the most rugged car available—and it could be strengthened further to cope with primitive Russian roads. (Nearly forty years later, in 1968, the Soviets still manufactured Model A engines for jeep-type vehicles.) Ford was planning to replace the Model A in the United States with the Ford V-8. The completion schedule for the Soviet factory allowed Ford to sell Model A tools and dies that would otherwise have been scrapped.

Henry Ford drew sharp criticism from American industrial leaders for contracting with communists and for abetting foreign competition. However, Ford understood the world market in a way that others did not. As he told *Nation's Business:*

> Russia is beginning to build. It makes little difference what theory is back of the real work, for in the long run facts will control. . . . This system of keeping certain nations dependent on others economically

must disappear. It is going to disappear. I have long been convinced that we shall never be able to build a balanced economic order in the world until every people has become as self-supporting as possible. . . . The adoption of high wages, low prices, and mass production in all countries is only a matter of time. Instead of reducing our foreign markets, it will serve to define them.[3]

Soviet representatives also approached the Austin Company. In 1927 the Austin Company had designed and erected the world's largest and most efficient automobile plant—the Pontiac Six factory for General Motors. The facility encompassed thirty-five acres of floor space. Austin had completed construction in just seven months. After the factory began production, General Motors announced "surprising price reductions—made possible by the efficiency and economies of the world's largest and finest motor car factory." Speed was the essence of Stalin's five year plan, and it was evident that no other builder could match Austin's performance. In an interview two years later, Wilbert Austin recalled his initial contacts with the Russians.

> I was not much impressed when the Soviet Government first brought up the matter of this contract in 1928. But I changed many of my ideas during the following winter when a delegation of Russian officials visited us after an inspection trip to some of this country's automobile centers. There were Communist officials in that delegation drawing $125 a month[,] which is the party salary limit, whose abilities would command twenty times that sum in this country.
>
> I was much impressed by their open-mindedness. I have met many members of European delegations, over here to try to get the secret of our industrial supremacy; but none that I have ever met grasped the idea so quickly or so completely as those Russians. They have no industrial traditions to bind them. They are starting fresh, building up with nothing to tear down.[4]

George Bryant took charge of the detailed negotiations that followed. He had supervised construction of the Pontiac Six factory for the Austin Company, and he was now the company's vice president and sales manager. After

Wilbert J. Austin (1876–1940). *The Austin Company Archives*

Henry Ford signed his contract, Bryant and an assistant, Fred Coleman, joined a tour sponsored by a group known as the American-Russian Chamber of Commerce to view a wide range of Soviet industrial enterprises. Parting from the tour, they took rooms in the Grand Hotel on Revolutionary Square in Moscow to pursue direct negotiations. On July 25 Bryant made a formal proposal to V. V. Kuibyshev, chairman of the VSNH, by which the Austin Company would design the automobile factory for $250,000 and supervise its construction, for 4 percent of the construction cost.[5]

The project envisioned the erection of a vast Russian facility—the most daunting challenge ever considered by Austin. The proposed factory complex would enclose twice the space of the Pontiac Six facility. Although the assembly line itself would be smaller, the Soviet factory would not simply assemble cars but also manufacture, on site, nearly every component required for their assembly. The project included a foundry, forge shop, pressed steel shop, spring shop, and warehouses. It required a new city for the workers to be employed, also to be built by Austin—apartment blocks, water, sewage, food processing facilities, laundries, etc. It required a powerhouse sufficient to supply heat and electricity for both factory and city. Austin proposed to design the complex and oversee construction at the site. This would include guiding Russian supervisors who would train peasant laborers in modern construction skills. The Soviets wanted the job completed in two years.

As negotiations continued, Bryant communicated by telegraph with Wilbert Austin and other managers in Cleveland. "We have seen nothing but peaceful, ambitious people," Bryant told a newspaper reporter. "Their economic progress is almost beyond belief; yet their plans are far beyond their accomplishments." In another interview, Wilbert Austin gave an account of the negotiations.

Before Mr. Bryant opened the first conference in Russia he made a direct statement of the position of our company: "I am an American business man," he told the Soviet officials. "We believe in the principles of capitalism and in legitimate profits from honest business transactions, and would not be interested in any other basis of negotiation." Mr. Bryant was assured that his attitude was understood and expected. . . .

We had thought that the Soviet system of government might make dealings difficult. The various activities of the Government are conducted by bureaus. The bureau with which we are dealing is known as Autostroy, and its responsibility is the building of automobile plants. . . . There are many men who have an industrial background. Others have not, but our experience convinced us that all had been chosen because of their ability. Their energy, insight, and ability to plunge right to the heart of a problem and drive the best possible bargain, compare favorably with the methods of business executives in any country.

The women of Monastryka wash laundry in the village pond. This village would be torn down to make way for the new factory. *The Austin Company Archives*

The negotiations, instead of being with individuals, were practically all conducted in committee. These conferences often lasted far into the night, and the committee members fought point for point for their own advantage, but there was never any lack of courtesy or any effort to take undue advantage. Engineers and automobiles were placed at the disposal of our representatives, and they had full cooperation in getting at all essential facts.

The selection of the site for the city was made after Mr. Bryant and a number of executives of Autostroy had gone carefully over three proposed locations. After a day of inspection, an evening was spent in discussing the three sites. The chief executive of the bureau listened to all the arguments and in the morning gave his decision. As it happened, the site he approved was the one favored by Mr. Bryant.[6]

There was a surprising synergy between the company, which practiced "the Austin Method," and the revolutionary government. Austin's capacity to build rapidly and assure quality depended upon "undivided responsibility" for all aspects of a project and upon open, person-to-person relationships with clients willing to settle disputes swiftly without recourse to legal evasions. Austin presented an unblemished history of integrity and competence. Clients were asked to invest trust and respect, in addition to money, so Austin might move the project along swiftly on the client's behalf.

The Western business community did not trust communists, yet the Soviets wished to acquire Western technology quickly. To do so they had to find firms willing to risk a relationship of trust across ideological, cultural, and physical distances. In return, the Soviets needed to demonstrate that they could work with capitalists in a responsible manner. In a project such as this, problems would occur that no contract could anticipate. The story of how these problems were resolved and how the project was completed is one of the most intriguing in modern industrial history.

The Soviets had to choose trustworthy partners and then rely upon them because they were desperate to move forward. The Austin Company chose to trust because that was its "method," derived from its Methodist roots. It was the company's experience that when a firm acts with integrity and demands respect, it inspires trust. Frederick Van Fleet, who conducted the interview with W. J. Austin that has been cited, noted an example of this.

On the matter of fair dealing and trustworthiness there is one incident related by Mr. Austin which illustrates admirably the attitude of the Russians. As the negotiations in Moscow were drawing to a close, a memorandum of agreement was drawn up. The Americans went over it in detail and discovered an error which would cost their company several thousand dollars. But before this could be called to their attention, the Russians announced that they had discovered it themselves and that

George Bryant leans forward to sign the Autostroy contract. *The Austin Company Archives*

the agreement was being rewritten so that the error might be corrected. The Austin representatives employed their own interpreter as a check on the official interpreter, but there was never a time in the whole negotiation when any discrepancy was found.[7]

On August 23, 1929, Soviet negotiators received two cables from America. One, from the Austin Company, gave George Bryant formal authority to sign the proposed contract on the company's behalf. The second, from I. A. Poliakov, head of the Soviet's foreign trade office in New York, warned against the Austin proposal and urged delay until September, when another American builder, Morris Kahn, might bring a less costly proposal to Moscow. Poliakov warned against the great sum to be paid to Austin. The problem was not the 4 percent commission but Austin's estimate of the total construction cost, which, in Poliakov's opinion, should be 25 to 30 percent less.[8] Nevertheless, Autostroy and George Bryant signed the momentous agreement that same day.

The contract obligated the Austin Company to provide planning, architecture, engineering, and supervision. The Soviets were to furnish the materials and the labor, but responsibility for construction rested with the Austin Company until the job was completed. The Austin Company agreed to prepare drawings in eight months, to begin construction on May 1, 1930, and to complete construction fifteen months later. The cost of construction was initially estimated at forty million dollars. This, combined with the thirty million promised to Ford for its assembly line, parts, and training, made the undertaking the largest foreign-assisted project yet attempted by the Soviet government; it was also the largest project that the Austin Company had ever attempted. Payments to Austin were to be made monthly from Soviet gold reserves on deposit in the Chase National Bank in New York. By the time the work was completed, changes and additions were to raise the construction cost to sixty million dollars—nearly a billion in today's currency—but the Austin Company would collect far less than 4 percent of this amount.

Two months after the signing of this contract, on October 29, 1929, the speculative bubble of capitalist prosperity burst as a wave of panic selling engulfed the New York Stock Exchange. America, and then the world, slid toward the Great Depression. Few profitable contracts for industrial construction were awarded during the next decade. But the Austin Company already had before it the most challenging project, and potentially the most profitable, in its history.

3

"IN A FRIENDLY WAY"

Both the Austin Company and Autostroy set sail upon uncharted waters when they signed their contract on August 23, 1929. Language of key passages in the contract made it plain that there was little alternative to mutual trust: "If . . . there shall arise any controversy or difficulty the parties hereto shall settle them by mutual efforts, in a friendly way. . . . None of the parties hereto has the right to appeal to the court."[1]

Indeed, there was no court of law that both parties would have trusted. Instead, they set up a system of binding arbitration: each side could appoint an arbitrator, and these two would agree upon a third arbitrator. Alternatively, the parties agreed to call upon the Association of Swedish Engineers for binding arbitration, and that association agreed to serve if requested.

The official correspondence between the Austin Company and Autostroy from 1929 through 1931, recently released by the Nizhny Novgorod Regional Archives, reveals a litany of complaints and disputes as this difficult project moved forward swiftly but erratically, with many changes along the way. There were times when one side or the other came close to canceling the contract. Yet every dispute was in fact resolved without outside assistance, "in a friendly way."

In the United States this huge contract with the communists was national news. The Austin Company historian, Martin Greif, wrote, "Upon his return from Moscow aboard the *Berengaria*, Bryant was greeted by newsmen who immediately—and erroneously—reported that 'the new city [would] be named "Austingrad" in honor of the builders,' an unfounded claim never considered seriously by the Russians or by The Austin Company."[2] Within a year, Austin personnel would learn that—for Soviet political purposes—the American presence in Russia would be kept as inconspicuous as possible.

When the contract was signed a great deal remained to be determined concerning the size and composition of the factory. A supplemental agreement signed on October 30 increased the proposed capacity of the plant from a hundred thousand vehicles a year to 120,000. The contract featured an elaborate schedule of commitments by both sides to perform tasks by specified dates so that construction might begin on May Day of 1930 and be completed fifteen months later. Subsequent tardiness would occasion many letters of complaint from both sides.

The contract stipulated a complex formula for calculating fees to be paid to the Austin Company based upon the value of work in place, including the value of labor performed by Russian workers. The contract presumed that most materials would be purchased in the United States and shipped to Nizhny Novgorod. As was typical in Austin contracts, the company agreed to penalties for late compliance and was promised bonuses for such services as procuring materials at prices lower than Soviet agents could negotiate. However, all of this complexity proved to be unworkable. After two months of actual construction, the two sides negotiated a second supplemental agreement, signed July 18, 1930, that set fixed fees for Austin's work: $250,000 for design and engineering, plus nine hundred thousand for on-site supervision of construction. In addition, the Austin Company probably received small fees for special services.

The contract forthrightly placed the Austin Company in charge of construction: "All construction and installation works as stipulated by this agreement are to be carried out under direct supervision of the CONCERN [The Austin Company] by the AUTOSTROY or any other Soviet organization which the AUTOSTROY will find necessary to invite to perform construction works. In this case the AUTOSTROY is the party fully responsible to the CONCERN for the carrying out of this Agreement."[3] Implementing this provision and maintaining Austin authority on the construction site would prove frustrating. The Austin Company had secured, in an appendix to the contract, a promise from Autostroy not to attempt to hire engineers or supervisors away from the company or to negotiate with such specialists behind the back of the company. This was fortunate, for Soviet officials would be tempted, on occasion, to solicit Austin personnel.

As soon as Autostroy signed contracts with both the Ford Motor Company and the Austin Company, Soviet specialists were dispatched to Ford's giant River Rouge plant in Dearborn, Michigan, where Model A Fords were assembled. For six years Autostroy maintained an office in the Rouge plant complex. Some specialists worked with Ford counterparts to determine the basic requirements for the new facility; others studied production techniques that they would need to master in order to operate the Russian factory. Automotive historian Robert Scoon reports, "In April 1930 one hundred and twenty Russians were in Dearborn studying Ford methods."[4]

Eventually the Depression created a pool of unemployed American workers. Henry Ford began to discharge experienced assembly-line workers and to replace them with younger workers, who were paid reduced wages. Workers responded with renewed attempts to organize and strike. Harold Evans, in *The American Century*, reports that Henry Ford turned over labor relations "to Harry Bennett, a short, redheaded thug with ties to the mob who ran a 'Service Department' of spies and goons. . . . Violence was the Bennett-Ford answer to any expression of grievance. In 1932 they crushed a Communist demonstration in a fracas at Dearborn's River Rouge plant, in which four were shot dead."[5]

Historians of the Ford Motor Company, Mira Wilkins and Frank Ernest Hill, note that communist engineers from Autostroy lent no support to the workers. "In 1932 in the midst of the depression when communist hunger marchers stormed the Rouge plant, the Russians blandly watched the demonstration from the capitalist citadel. The mob flung rocks at the Gate Four office building [where the Russians worked], and Harry Bennett wisecracked, 'You're stoning your own fellows up there.' But the Russian engineers—indifferent to the political implications—stayed on to continue their study of Ford methods

Fred Coleman (*right*), accompanied by his driver and interpreter, rides a Russian *drozhky,* which, as well as Russian-built Fords, were used to taxi officials around during the construction period. *The Austin Company Archives*

at first hand."[6] The Soviet engineers in the River Rouge office may not have been "indifferent," but they were surely under orders to stick to their jobs.

While Soviet specialists traveled to the Ford Motor Company in the United States, the Austin Company assigned two engineers to remain in Russia through the autumn and winter of 1929 as liaison with Moscow officials and with Soviet crews beginning site preparations in Nizhny Novgorod. By November, with the Russian winter closing in, the memos of these engineers to Autostroy were filled with complaints. No work had begun on the housing for Austin engineers due to arrive at the site the following April. Construction of docks on the river and roads to the factory site was behind schedule, and insufficient building materials had been off-loaded. Since no steam pile-driver had been secured, despite repeated requests, "they are still driving piles in the same old way [manually] and as a result only a small amount of dock will be ready for spring use."

Difficulties were emerging between the Austin Company and "Metallostroy," the Soviet organization that hired and supervised construction labor, and these problems would intensify in the year ahead. The minutes of a November 21 conference with Autostroy officials reveal that one resident Austin engineer exploded with frustration: "Mr. Coleman emphasized that in case the Metallostroy people do not radically reform and change their methods, the results will disastrously affect the construction work of the spring 1930."

During the early decades of the twentieth century, most American construction companies resisted trade unions that bargained collectively to achieve better wages and working conditions for their members. The Austin Company was the exception, for Wilbert Austin willingly signed contracts with the principal construction unions in the United States. These unions were organized according to skilled crafts, and they generally represented their workers without pursuing radical political agendas. The contracts spelled out work rules, which were understood by both sides. Since Austin had solicited union contracts and paid its workers well, the unions were generally eager to resolve disputes with dispatch and to provide Austin construction sites with skilled and cooperative workforces.

Metallostroy, and the Communist Party cadres that supervised it behind the scenes, were still experimenting with styles of labor organization appropriate to their postrevolutionary situation. Efficiency might be compromised by political requirements. Decision making was tedious and, from Austin's perspective, obscure. Committees with authority were hidden from view, and Austin managers were expected to deal with Metallostroy through Autostroy officials. For example, while Autostroy engineers at Dearborn, working with their Ford counterparts, were providing the Austin Company in Cleveland with requirements for the industrial buildings, conceptual development for the adjacent Worker's City had been placed in the hands of Metallostroy, which had given no specifications to Austin engineers.

In January 1930, the All-Union Automobile and Tractor Association (VATO), the agency responsible for this branch of the Soviet economy, summoned Autostroy and Metallostroy to report on their progress in Nizhny Novgorod; it witnessed instead an "animal fight" of "petty accusations" between these two trusts. VATO rebuked Metallostroy for refusing to comply with a "categorical order" to provide Autostroy with a variety of construction materials. The problem, as Kurt Schultz explains in a recent essay, was endemic to Soviet efforts to force economic expansion and to resolve scarcities of materials or labor without resorting to free markets.

Avtostroi had calculated the costs of supplies and was unwilling to pay more. Metallostroi had other ideas and demanded that Avtostroi buy a larger amount of goods at prices that would help Metallostroi meet its production and distribution targets. Without intervention from Moscow, Metallostroi would have been in an impregnable position because, like other supply and production entities, it was barraged with more orders than it could possibly fulfill. The abolition of capitalist market relations notwithstanding, Metallostroi enjoyed a seller's market, which under "socialism" allowed it to act "like a feudal prince"; as long as its own plan was fulfilled it could "treat the needs of its consumers with the arrogance of a baron" [as one Russian newspaper commented].[7]

VATO required Autostroy and Metallostroy to sign an elaborate protocol intended to structure their relationships with each other and with the Austin Company. The agreement obligated Metallostroy to learn American construction methods and to cooperate closely with Austin specialists, whose instructions and orders were to be considered "binding." Nevertheless a February article in *Izvestiya,* under the headline "Defective Works on Nizhny Novgorod Auto-Plant Factory Construction Site," scolded Autostroy and Metallostroy for competing rather than cooperating: "American speed of work is replaced by Nizhny Novgorod tempo." A March article in *Za industrializatsiyu* complained, "The plan is not fulfilled. The slowness of materials procurement is menacing." In April the same newspaper—reviewing preparations for the imminent arrival of Austin engineers, who would begin construction on May Day—reported disorder everywhere, especially in the organization of supplies, transportation, and labor, as well as the utilization of machinery.[8]

Meanwhile, in downtown Nizhny Novgorod, Ford engineers were struggling with similar problems. Their contract called for a prototype assembly line to be set up in a warehouse building so that Soviet managers and workers might obtain practical experience. All the tools, dies, jigs, and fixtures for a small assembly line had been shipped to Nizhny Novgorod, as well as crates of unassembled cars and trucks. Soviet engineers who had been trained in Dearborn erected the line. However, when Ford's supervising engineer arrived on New Year's Day, 1930, he found that the temporary factory was not running. "It couldn't—only a short survey showed me that it wouldn't run."

Ford engineers advocated "abolishing piece work, raising wages, and clearing out the bureaucratic confusion that paralyzed the factory like a disease."

Despite these problems, the first Ford vehicles rolled off this prototype assembly line in February. "Droves of Russians visited the plant to watch the miracle of continuous production.... They regarded the accomplishment as mainly their own and made dazzling predictions for the future." This line was designed to produce twenty vehicles a day, and indeed, during 1930 all of 3,714 cars and pickup trucks were assembled there.[9]

Tensions mounted in the United States during the spring of 1930 between Autostroy engineers in Dearborn and Austin Company engineers in Cleveland. Austin had established a special engineering department for this relationship. Design work on the many industrial buildings required a hundred drafting tables and even more employees, many of them hired for this specific task. "Fast-track" construction techniques, for which the Austin Company was famous, required the client to present a clear statement of needs and allow the builder some flexibility in meeting those needs. On other jobs, Austin would pour foundations while its engineers were still preparing drawings for the building itself. The Autostroy contract presumed that engineering would conform to American standards and that Autostroy would order critical building components designed to American standards and have them shipped to Russia.

Autostroy engineers in Dearborn were disappointed by the incompleteness of Austin's preliminary designs—"insufficient and unsatisfactory presentation of the structures," they called it. They demanded more detail. As designs evolved each side recommended changes to which the other objected. The design of the Foundry Building in particular—the heaviest and most difficult construction proposed for the site—was delayed for months by such conflict.

As the deepening worldwide depression reduced Soviet export earnings and shrunk the Soviet Union's hard-currency reserves, Autostroy proposed shopping for building materials on the world market in order to secure them at lower cost. However, European components drew upon different engineering traditions and were configured in metric units, so Austin managers objected strenuously. Such substitutions, they claimed, might require that buildings be reengineered. This would take additional time and cost extra.

In April 1930 Autostroy withheld a scheduled payment to the Austin Company because of inadequate progress. "The none-too-good existing relations between the Austin Company and ourselves was aggravated by our withholding the $50,000." This observation and other details concerning these disputes are found in a thirteen-page English-language memo from Autostroy officials in Dearborn to their superiors in Nizhny Novgorod.[10] (The Autostroy staff wrote in English in this instance because they lacked sufficient Russian-language typists.)

There followed a blizzard of angry correspondence between Austin and Autostroy, filled with charges, demands, and excuses. At last Wilbert Austin contacted the Amtorg Trading Company, the Soviet foreign trade agency that in fact paid the bills. Amtorg representatives agreed to meet in Cleveland on April 25 with senior managers from Autostroy and from the Austin Company.

No minutes of this conference have been preserved, but one can imagine the scene. Wilbert Austin presided as host and also, of course, as the party seeking the delayed payment for services. Autostroy representatives laid out a litany of complaints. Nevertheless Wilbert—who had developed the "Austin Method" of swift construction under undivided responsibility, and who embodied the absolute integrity upon which this method depended—was able to guide the discussion back to the fundamental needs of both sides. They were committed to cooperate with each other so the vast project could move forward successfully. "At that time," Autostroy would report following the conference, "it looked as if a really strenuous effort was being made by the Austin Company to complete the work." The Amtorg representatives present understood the high priority that Joseph Stalin placed upon this project, and they were not preoccupied by the details of engineering disputes, so before the meeting concluded they announced a decision that overruled and perplexed their Autostroy comrades. "Mr. Bagdonov," Autostroy would report, "had for some special reason decided that it would be beneficial for all concerned to have this payment made."[11]

The Austin Company, certainly, had no choice but to go forward. A month earlier, fifteen Austin Company mangers and engineers—five of them accompanied by their wives and two by children—had set sail for Germany, from where they would proceed by train to Moscow and on to Nizhny Novgorod. They arrived April 20, five days before the Cleveland conference.

My parents were the youngest in this group. My father had graduated from engineering school just three years earlier. He would serve as assistant superintendent for the construction of the Worker's City—work that posed fewer technical challenges than the industrial construction nearby.

Though least in seniority, Allan Austin was the son of the company president. In a steady stream of letters to his father, Wilbert, Allan would supplement the official information being passed to Cleveland by his superiors with more personal and intimate reporting on day-to-day life. Wilbert Austin retained these letters in a leather ring-binder stamped "SPECIAL REPORTS." Lost from view over time, these letters were presented to this author in 1998 by a woman who had assisted Allan Austin as his personal secretary during the decades following World War II.

These remarkable letters form the backbone of the Russian narrative. Allan Austin wrote his first letter on his twenty-fifth birthday.

United States Lines, April 1, 1930

Dearest Mother & Dad—

. . . Our trip to date has been very smooth and calm. Sunday and Monday were particularly so, and today there is a gentle swell and a few white caps. We are both good sailors and are eating regularly and heartily; but I spoiled the record by coming down with grippe Saturday night and spent most of Sunday in bed.

As you gathered from my shouted message at the dock, we are honored by the presence of Aimee Semple McPherson [a Los Angeles evangelist, flamboyant and notorious] and her daughter Roberta. I was greatly disappointed that I was unable to get up Sunday morning to hear her conduct the services, but Margretta went and heard the usual hokum. . . .

There is a party of 24 men and women bound for Tomsk, Siberia, on a coal mining project. So we have quite a boat load of prospective Russians.

Allan

4

"SPIRIT AND ABILITY"

Central Hotel, Berlin, Wed., April 16, 1930

Dearest Mother and Dad—

It is now 4:00, and at 6:30 we start on the real journey. All of the final arrangements have been made here—tickets, visas, and baggage checking. Now we wait for the train.

The entire group is in good spirits. We are "going in" feeling well and confident and with a strong sense of Austin spirit and ability. This opportunity to serve the Russian people is a privilege of which we hope to take full advantage.

Allan

The Austin party traveled in a private sleeping car that served as their hotel for the remainder of the journey. When the group arrived in Moscow on April 17 they encountered logistical confusion: according to a report filed by the head of the Soviet Interpreters Bureau, Autostroy had dispatched only one automobile to the station to meet the large party. The next night the group

АВТОЗАВОД
Н-НОВГОРОД
СССР

R-22

attended the Bolshoy Theater for a performance of *Eugene Onegin*. Then they were taken to a different railway station, for trains departing to Nizhny Novgorod. "It turned out that their sleeping car was missing at the station and came there only at 4 A.M. of April 19. So Austin specialists and their families had to spend that night (from 11:30 P.M. till 4 A.M.) at the station buffet, and, as the buffet works only until 2 A.M., we had to ask an agent on duty for assistance."[1] They did not depart Moscow until the following evening. My parents had brought a chess set to pass the time in such situations. However, as Margretta told the story years later, she checkmated Allan so consistently that he soon refused to play against her.

Finally, on the morning of April 20, the group arrived in Nizhny Novgorod and was taken to the Russia Hotel. Apparently the beds were infested with fleas or bedbugs, so badly that some weeks later when three Austin Company families were required to spend another night in downtown Nizhny Novgorod, the wives refused to return to this hotel and insisted upon sleeping in their car. Allan Austin reported none of these difficulties to his father, Wilbert.

Nijni-Novgorod, April 23, 1930

Dearest Mother and Dad —

This is the first opportunity I have had to write you since we arrived here on the 20th. We have accommodations in the "Russia" hotel here until our housing is completed at the job. We expect to move out there in two or three days. . . .

The chief difficulty with our stay in Nijni is the time consumed in getting to and from the job. It takes about an hour each way, sometimes more. Autostroy furnishes us with cars to go and come in—Model A Fords!

At this particular season of the year the pontoon bridge is down and we must use the ferry, which is rather slow. This bridge is down only

Left: This table-sized model of the planned Autostroy factory was built by The Austin Company in 1930. Austin made handsome building models for its clients, photographed them well, and used the photos in advertising campaigns. In numerous publications (even in the official Austin Company history) this has been erroneously identified as an aerial photograph of the completed factory. *The Austin Company Archives*

Below: This 1929 panorama of Nizhny Novgorod shows the busy mouth of the Oka River as it flows into the Volga at the far left. On the bluff above that confluence stands the city's kremlin, the old fortress, and to the right is the temporary pontoon bridge that allowed vehicles to cross the Oka on their way to the Autostroy project. George Bryant wrote home about this scene: "This city is very beautiful, located on a bank about 400 feet high—white buildings with red roofs against green grass, and the wide river flowing at the foot of the bank with many white boats moving about. This is the river and this is the city where sturgeon fish are caught, from which they get the caviar that is so famous." *GAZ Museum of History*

With good humor Allan photographed the banners that the Soviets hung in the American Village. The top banner reads, "Long Live the Soviet Union, the Fatherland of the Working People of the Entire World!" and the one below it exhorts, "Long Live the First of May, a Glorious Demonstration of Revolutionary Forces of the Young Proletariat!" *Allan Austin Album*

about two months or less, while the ice breaks up on the Oka. A new concrete bridge is planned and construction is to start immediately. The materials are already assembled. . . .

Margretta and Mrs. Davis are jumping right into the language and already have over 100 words at their command. I have had so little time that I have learned practically nothing since I came.

Allan

Before the official start of construction on May Day, 1930, the Austin engineers and their families moved to the "American Village," which had been prepared for them near the construction site. Groundbreaking ceremonies for the factory were in fact delayed until the second of May so dignitaries from Moscow could join the festivities.

Friday, May 2, 1930

Dear Dad—

Today marked the actual start of construction work on the Automobile plant at Nijni Novgorod. It was attended by considerable celebration and ceremony and was quite impressive. It was part of the general May Day festivities, and train-loads of people came out from Nijni especially for the occasion. I should judge that there were five thousand spectators.

A platform was erected from which numerous short speeches were made. At the beginning and end of each, the "International" was played. By personal count it was played at least 25 times. Then followed the laying of the first piece of rubble-stone foundation. This is a change from our original plan, on account of materials. The old, solid, aproned stone-masons looked as though they had worked on the Parthenon. Certain trades such as this one are well developed here. Building log houses and timber work is another. . . .

Mr. Bryant and Miter and Wolfe returned this morning from Moscow where they saw the May Day celebration, which of course was the big one. These people seem solidly and actively behind their government, and taking a real interest in all the activity and progress which is going on. The group at the celebration today was the most representative and well-dressed that we have seen.

We are looking forward keenly to your visit to us this summer, and feel that you will be pleased with our quarters and surroundings here. The weather so far has been cool, and sometimes cold, but today Mr. Makarovsky said that in two weeks the country will be beautiful and spring-like. . . .

Allan

Laying the First Stone

The First Stone

The only surviving photos of this moment. *Allan Austin Album*

Makarovsky was apparently the Autostroy representative on the Worker's City construction site, where Allan Austin served as assistant superintendent for the Austin Company. Allan was to mention him often as they worked together.

George Bryant continued to handle sensitive negotiations in Moscow, while H. A. Miter supervised overall construction at the site. In the large, single-story engineering office, American and Russian engineers worked side by side, assisted by interpreters—primarily young women from the Moscow School of Foreign Languages. The Austin engineers could do little without assistance from these interpreters, but since the women journeyed from downtown Nizhny Novgorod each morning, they often arrived late. Frustrated by such delays, Miter soon exploded.

May 10, 1930

Autostroy, Nijni Novgorod. . . .

We wish to bring forcefully to your attention the serious condition existing with regard to Interpreters. At this writing, 10 A.M. of this date, the entire force of Interpreters and Typists who travel to and from Nijni each morning have not yet arrived at this office to start work.

We have four of our men waiting in this office right now that have been waiting since 8 A.M. to start work in the field. You can appreciate that without Interpreters they can do nothing, consequently they must wait until Interpreters arrive.

This condition has existed since the first day of our arrival and has grown worse. We are making formal complaint and insist that you make immediate provision to have a complete force of Interpreters here at this office at 8 A.M. every morning. In order to accomplish the work we have to do, we must have this co-operation. . . .

H. A. Miter[2]

Although the interpreters were students of English, learning the technical language of construction was a challenge. Years later Allan Austin would recall, "During the time I was on the job I had a succession of these girls and I had to train each one. I could tell her the name of a piece of equipment, a joist or whatever, in English; then she would turn to a Russian engineer for the corresponding word in Russian. After I had been through about three of these gals I knew enough technical Russian to work without an interpreter."

Yet, as the people with whom the Austin personnel could converse, the interpreters played an important role in social and political orientation. My parents, themselves young, identified with these young people. Margretta, who considered herself an intellectual, found opportunities for stimulating conversation with the interpreters that were not available elsewhere. So the views

of these young, enthusiastic communists—and the information they furnished—made an impression upon this American couple with capitalist and Christian backgrounds.

The Soviets had replaced the Christian week with a new rotation: four days of work followed by one day of rest. Allan described a rest day in this letter addressed to his parents and also to Margretta's. Since he composed on a typewriter, it was easy to include a carbon copy. (Note, as on previous page, that in the 1930s the city name was transliterated into English as "Nijni," rather than "Nizhny," which generally is preferred today.)

May 11, 1930

Dear Families—

I'll write to both of you at once and tell you some things that we did today. It was a Rest Day for me and most of the Austin men, so as usual we were very busy. A Rest Day is such in name only so far, for there are

Seventeen Austin engineers pose before their construction office in the American Village. Allan Austin, the youngest, is in the first row, just to the right of the man with cap and cigarette. Fred Coleman, who worked in Russia for nine months before construction began, stands tall at the back, his eyes shaded by his hat. Harry Miter, the bald project supervisor with the white tie, stands fourth from the right. Chet Appleton, who assisted Miter as chief engineer, squats before him, hat in hand. To Appleton's left is Bill Wolfe, who worked in Moscow on the design for the Workers' City. Walter Baggaley, the tall man at the far left, supervised construction of the factory. Harry Sprackling, with bowtie and pipe, is beside him; he supervised construction of the Worker's City, assisted by Allan. *The Austin Company Archives*

When Austin Company engineers moved to the "American Village" at the construction site, exterior stucco had not yet been applied. Allan and Margretta occupied a ground-floor apartment (in this photo a telephone pole brace bisects their window). After the Austin engineers completed their work, the village housed Ford Motor Company technicians, and in subsequent years various groups of foreign workers, including Walter Reuther and Victor Reuther, lived here as well. *The Austin Company Archives*

so many things we all want to do and buy and see that we must avail ourselves of every opportunity.

At 10:30 a bus came to the house and ten of us piled in. We drove to Kanavenaugh, the town on this side of the river opposite Nijni, and were deposited at the market which was quite busy and large today. Certain days are more important than others in these street markets. The market is made up partly of stores and established booths along the streets, and partly of individuals selling belongings of their own of every description. These people make the market very interesting and varied from day to day. It was the first time Margretta and I had been in together and we wanted a number of things.

First we found some quaint little wooden bowls and boxes of various sizes, handmade and decorated. Then we picked up two brass candlesticks to adorn our very large mantle-piece. These for a ruble each. Then Margretta found some linen for dish cloths, also handmade, several meters of that. One must carry his market basket for there are no wrappers and bags are unknown. We got twenty eggs in a bowl we had brought for the purpose. Eggs are somewhat cheaper in the market, about 65 cents for ten.

Our principal purchase here was a samovar. We have been looking for a nice one ever since we arrived. It has a very handsome design and proportions, is finished in nickel, is in good repair with all the parts present and is about 12 years old. The construction is very solid and workmanship seems good. We paid forty rubles. . . .

Several of us, with the interpreter, then took a ferry to Nijni. It was not so good a day in their market, but I got a Russian shirt which buttons up the side of the neck and has black embroidery on it. The color is dark red and the effect is rather pretty. Then, in a government store, Margretta bought a large scarf of cashmere with gay flowers on it, so that we could drape one of our trunks which still forms a principal piece of furniture in our living room.

The afternoon ended in a splurge of luxury with Appleton and myself getting haircuts. The Russians are excellent barbers, some of the world's best we are told. They did very well by us. Styles in haircutting vary between the wildest extremes. On one side of me was a kindly old gentleman having his rather long hair and full beard trimmed—with a woman barber doing the work, by the way. On the other side was a young man saying good-bye forever to his splendid head of hair by having the barber

clip his head closely and then shave it absolutely clean and bare of a single hair. This is a popular style among younger men. It looks strange when one is not accustomed to seeing it.

We decided to take a boat home, going up the Oka to the job dock and walking the mile from there to our houses. None of us had taken this ride on the river and it was very pretty. . . .

We both send all of you much love and the assurance that we are quite well and as happy as we can be so far from home.

Allan

Through my childhood this small, elegant samovar, fifteen inches high, occupied a place of honor in our living room. I still have it on display, along with antique brass-and-enamel icons that Margretta purchased.

Chet Appleton, mentioned above and often referred to by the nickname "App," was the chief engineer. This was the second-highest position on the Austin Company team. However, his job was not to supervise the other engineers—indeed, Appleton was the only member of the team who lacked an engineering degree. As was customary on an Austin Company construction site, the job of the number-two man was to anticipate difficulties and attempt to resolve them before they affected the tight construction schedule. Appleton was chosen for this job because of his remarkable ability to win the respect of others and to inspire their best efforts. "App" was Allan Austin's closest friend on the American team.

May 18, 1930

Dearest Mother and Dad—

One of our most difficult problems here is getting the kind and variety of food we need. For us there is no actual shortage of food, but the choice is quite limited and the prices rather high. Few fresh vegetables yet, for the spring is so late. Poor meat: I got a live chicken yesterday; they are hard to buy because this is the laying season and the peasants do not raise chickens for eating. Fortunately, our maid can clean it. The bread is rather poor, even the best, and the black bread is uneatable. So we must return to first principles and use a lot of ingenuity to think up dishes that can be made from limited choice.

Margretta has certainly risen to the occasion. She is one of the foremost cooks in the outfit. It is rather surprising that some women who have never done this sort of thing before seem better able to adapt themselves, and others who have often been in construction camps are having the hardest time. Margretta's pie-making ability is unchallenged, and she is daily doing successfully what she had never tried before. . . . Tonight we had chicken pie and sponge cake with fig dressing. . . .

It is really too early to try to pass any kind of judgment on the Russians and their new social structure. It is quite apparent, as I presumed before I came, that in many places there are wide discrepancies between theory and practice. These discrepancies are not always apparent on the surface, but as we get better acquainted, especially with non-official people, we are able to hear more of the actual conditions and workings of the Soviets.

For example, a rigid food economy is enforced. Each family is allotted ¼ lb. of meat per day. There are also restrictions on bread, flour, and other foodstuffs, as well as a complete lack of many articles we would consider essential. Everywhere it is apparent that the best of *everything* produced in Russia is exported to obtain foreign credit. The natives take what is left. We are no exception to that export rule: while we can have plenty of what is available, the choice is limited and the quality inferior.

Allan could only glimpse the farming crisis that gripped the Soviet Union. The majority of Russians were agricultural peasants living in traditional villages with deep communal traditions. Nevertheless, Lenin and most Marxists had despised peasant society as "anarchic," "backward," "counter-revolutionary."[3] Lenin, and Joseph Stalin after him, saw traditional village cooperation and decision making, in which all peasants took part, as a threat to Communist Party control. Stalin struggled to impose novel collective structures under direct party supervision. These efforts disorganized agriculture and decreased production. Then poor crop weather in 1929 deepened the food crisis. Villages tried to retain food for their winter survival and seeds for spring planting, but Stalin placed higher priority upon feeding industrial workers and upon export sales to generate hard currency. As Lenin had done in 1918, Stalin launched a virtual war on his peasant population, seizing stores of grain and

Near the American Village, this beautiful church overlooked the village of Karpovka. These old houses were removed to make way for factory construction, but the church remained open throughout the Communist era. After Nizhny Novgorod was renamed Gorky, this Russian Orthodox church continued as one of the only three permitted to conduct services in Russia's industrial hub city. *Archives of Walter and Victor Reuther*

other provisions. To subvert village order, he tried to turn the poorest peasants against those with some stored provisions—he called those *"kulaks,"* or middle-class farmers, although in fact all were peasants with modest differences in fortune. Thousands of the most capable farmers were murdered during the pillaging of villages for stored food supplies. Vast numbers of horses and oxen, still required for plowing, were destroyed. At last, on March 2, 1930, Stalin released a letter, "Dizzy with Success," ordering a halt to this campaign. Soviet food production would continue to deteriorate, however, over the next two years.[4]

Allan Austin's letter continued.

The Church question doubtless will interest you. I guess you appreciate that the Church in Russia under the Czars was quite rotten from top to bottom, was a heavy burden on the people, and had little to offer them. There were and still are a very large number of churches, each costly and elaborate. Until quite recently the destruction of churches has been carried on quite extensively, until now one can see many foundations where churches had been. Materials are salvaged and used, rather dramatically and self-consciously, in the construction of modern factories, apartments, etc. There is little waste. It was the Government's privilege to disband a church, exile the priests, and destroy the building whenever it chose. Often the buildings are not destroyed but converted into schools, nurseries, hospitals, warehouses, or whatever use the structure can serve best in that particular community. And at present the Soviets have many more schools, nurseries, and hospitals than were ever established under the Czars.

In April 1930 an order issued from Moscow modified the powers of the government in such matters. Now the consent of the majority of members of the congregation is required before a church can be disbanded. And in the adjoining village of Karpovka there is a very pretty church which at present is in use, in its usual condition, and served by priests. So that if we chose, we could attend services any Sunday. So far as I know, there is now no molestation of this congregation, and it is doubtless typical of many other village and rural churches. The condition in cities is usually more severe and more truly Communistic. But the inertia of the large rural population is a very important factor. . . .

It is in the light of previous conditions that the present government appears most favorable. . . .

Allan

5

"THE FIRST COMMUNIST CITY IN THE WORLD"

May 15, 1930

Dear Dad—

. . . Our Worker's City is getting all lined up to go; temporary construction and tracks, etc., being well under way now, and final plans expected soon. I think that more work will be done on this development than on the industrial plant in the next few months, as we are not lacking in any of the principal materials. Our schedule starts one building every two days until 30 are started, and will enclose a building in about 60 days, and complete it in about 30 more. Probably 5000 men will be engaged directly in the erection of these buildings and of course many more in transporting, fabricating and otherwise preparing materials. We do as much manufacturing as building here, due to the raw state of materials. . . .

Allan

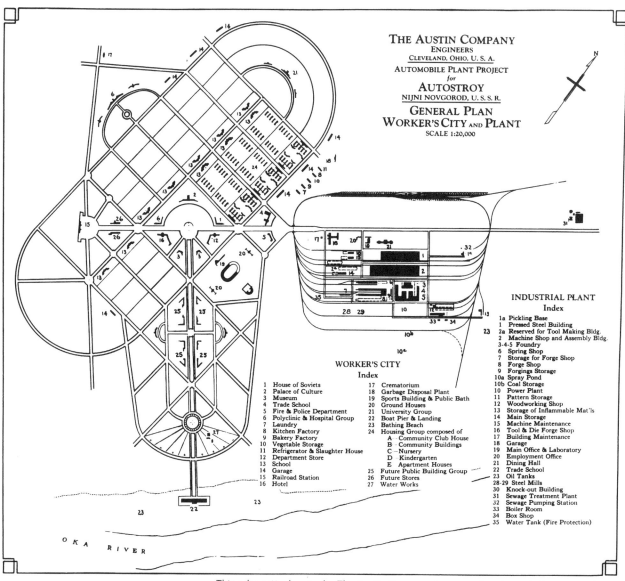

THE AUSTIN COMPANY
ENGINEERS
Cleveland, Ohio, U.S.A.
AUTOMOBILE PLANT PROJECT
for
AUTOSTROY
NIJNI NOVGOROD, U.S.S.R.
GENERAL PLAN
WORKER'S CITY and PLANT
SCALE 1:20,000

WORKER'S CITY
Index

1	House of Soviets	17	Crematorium
2	Palace of Culture	18	Garbage Disposal Plant
3	Museum	19	Sports Building & Public Bath
4	Trade School	20	Ground Houses
5	Fire & Police Department	21	University Group
6	Polyclinic & Hospital Group	22	Boat Pier & Landing
7	Laundry	23	Bathing Beach
8	Kitchen Factory	24	Housing Group composed of
9	Bakery Factory		A - Community Club House
10	Vegetable Storage		B - Community Buildings
11	Refrigerator & Slaughter House		C - Nursery
12	Department Store		D - Kindergarten
13	School		E - Apartment Houses
14	Garage	25	Future Public Building Group
15	Railroad Station	26	Future Stores
16	Hotel	27	Water Works

INDUSTRIAL PLANT
Index

1a	Pickling Base
1	Pressed Steel Building
2a	Reserved for Tool Making Bldg.
2	Machine Shop and Assembly Bldg.
3-4-5	Foundry
6	Spring Shop
7	Storage for Forge Shop
8	Forge Shop
9	Forgings Storage
10a	Spray Pond
10b	Coal Storage
10	Power Plant
11	Pattern Storage
12	Woodworking Shop
13	Storage of Inflammable Mat'ls
14	Main Storage
15	Machine Maintenance
16	Tool & Die Forge Shop
17	Building Maintenance
18	Garage
19	Main Office & Laboratory
20	Employment Office
21	Dining Hall
22	Trade School
23	Oil Tanks
28-29	Steel Mills
30	Knock-out Building
31	Sewage Treatment Plant
32	Sewage Pumping Station
33	Boiler Room
34	Box Shop
35	Water Tank (Fire Protection)

OKA RIVER

This schematic drawing by The Austin Company incorporates elements from several sources. Austin did the layout and design for the automobile plant. The dramatic layout for the Worker's City evolved from a competition among Soviet architectural institutions. Guided by this larger scheme, Austin completed the design of the initial apartment blocks (point 24) and placed service facilities (points 7–11) between the apartments and the factory. *The Austin Company Archives*

Excavation started today on the Worker's City. Our original schedule called for May 15, yet we are not so far behind as we might be. Mr. Makarovsky asked me if I was not proud to be starting construction of the first Communist City in the world, and I said that I was. It has the possibilities for being a momentous occasion. Whether it will be a "shot heard round the world," I do not know, but neither did the soldiers at Lexington or Concord.[1]

Anyway, we have an ambitious construction schedule ahead of us, and the Ruskies will be sweating to keep up with it. We too will be sweating to keep after them. Thirty buildings will be started within the next 60 days.

While the techniques of apartment construction were more familiar to Russian workers and supervisers than those of the complex factory construction nearby, the design of the Worker's City had proved to be the most challenging part of the project to date. The Austin Company had formal responsibility for this design and would willingly have laid out a community of serviceable buildings similar to those in an American city. However, to the Soviets this "first communist city" was far too significant to leave the design in the hands of capitalists. This was indeed the first city since the revolution to be erected from the ground up. It needed to represent, physically, the principles of that revolution. Although the Ford Motor Company and Autostroy had furnished the Austin Company with specifications for the factory, in this instance it was Metallostroy, the Communist Party, and leading Moscow intellectuals that took the keenest interest in design for the Worker's City.

Nevertheless, it was not altogether clear what the revolution implied for urban design. Joseph Stalin was eager for monumental construction projects, and these would become a Soviet tradition. Yet an architectural jury observed that "in spite of vivid discussion concerning 'socialist cities' planning, all these problems are far from final solution."[2] That jury gathered early in 1930 to evaluate Worker's City proposals that had been solicited from five leading Soviet architectural institutions.

Two principles emerged from the jury's review. One was a desire to "root out

The city plan proposed by the Moscow High Technical College featured an avenue for parades, a public square for arts and culture, and housing blocks linked by enclosed, elevated passageways. These features were carried into the final design. *GAZ Museum of History*

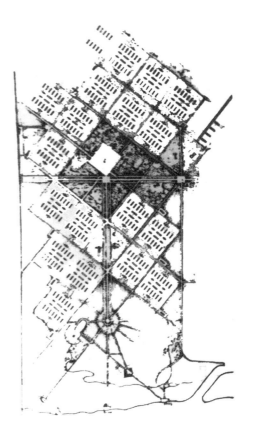

. . . norms and regulations . . . from pre-Revolutionary construction practice" that were determined to be alien to present social conditions. The other was to convey a "triangular" socialist reality, with "factory, living blocks, cultural zone" in dynamic relationship to one another.[3]

Eighteen students at the Moscow High Technical College developed the scheme that the jury particularly admired. Their proposal was among the least monumental, but it gave the most detailed attention to the care of children and to the linkage of housing with cultural and educational institutions.

From this point forward, design work for the Worker's City proceeded in an awkward collaboration among Autostroy, students from the Moscow High Technical College, and Austin Company engineers. On March 15 it was agreed that the small crew of Austin engineers in Moscow would supervise design, based upon the results of the architectural competition, with substantial assistance from Soviet architects, engineers, and draftsmen. Two weeks later the Austin Company complained that the promised assistance had not been forthcoming. Little design work had been accomplished, though weather for construction would soon be favorable and adequate materials to begin apartment construction were present at the site.

On April 14, just weeks before groundbreaking, Autostroy replied, "We handed over the detailed designing of the City to a special designing organization, which is working in close cooperation with Mr. Crosby [of the Austin Company, in Moscow]. Works are carried on in the augmented tempo and authors of the projects are taking their share in this work." Four days later the Austin Company reported that all parties had at last agreed upon a city layout. They also agreed upon the buildings to be erected during the first phase.

The city layout was grander than the Soviet students' original proposal and—when drawn by Austin engineers—it made a fine statement, one that was reproduced in articles around the world. However, most of the construction envisioned in that layout was postponed to the indefinite future. The particular buildings to be erected under the Austin contract drew from the students designs but were simplified somewhat and rendered more practical. For example, the cantilevered, glass-clad stairwells that the students had envisioned were replaced by simpler, but still handsome, masonry stairwells.

Yet design work continued to fall behind schedule. On May 11, just a week before ground was broken for the first apartment building, the Austin Company

The Austin Company compensated for the relative simplicity of its apartment designs by producing an elaborate scale model. Only the thirty apartment buildings in the foreground represent construction actually proposed; the buildings beyond those blocks were included for presentation only and were never part of the plan. Nevertheless, this photograph of the model was widely disseminated by Soviet officials, as well as by The Austin Company. In later years it was assumed to be an aerial photograph of the actual city. *The Austin Company Archives*

complained to Autostroy that its handful of Moscow engineers were doing most of the work, because Soviet help was insufficient. "On May 7th there were 10 Russian engineers and draftsmen working on the Workers City, seven on May 8th, and 5 men on May 9th. This is far from being a sufficient number of men to finish the plans on schedule for the buildings that are to be built in the first turn."[4] Austin requested six designing engineers, two electrical engineers, two heating engineers, two plumbing engineers, and fifteen draftsmen so work could be completed by July 1. Meanwhile, as was Austin's practice, excavation and foundation work would begin at the site.

As it turned out, the design for the initial buildings expressed both the Soviet vision for a new society and the practicality contributed by American engineers. After six months on the job, Allan Austin wrote an article about this design that was published in the *New York Times Magazine* on August 9, 1931. From a literary perspective, this is the finest essay that my father wrote during his lifetime. The description of the buildings and of their functions in the first half of the article is, I believe, the clearest, most perceptive in any language.

COMMUNISM BUILDS ITS CITY OF UTOPIA
Russia's Ideas of a Model Community Will Be Tested in a
Vast Project for Thousands of Families
by Allan S. Austin

On the north bank of the Oka River, a little more than six miles above its junction with the Volga at the historic market town of Nizhni Novgorod, is rising a new city for 60,000 inhabitants in which American engineers are translating into brick and concrete the social theories of the Soviet Government. Here in a land of forests—through which four centuries ago the traders were floating their rich cargoes of furs—the old Russia, the new Russia, and modern America have themselves flowed together like rivers.

The new city, carved out of what a year or two ago was almost wilderness, will be Communist Russia's conception of what a community ought to be. If it succeeds it will affect the future mode of life of the 150,000,000 people now inhabiting the Soviet Republics. On that score as well as because of the sheer magnitude of the enterprise it is second to no physical undertaking now under way in Russia. Here we see concretely expressed the theories of Communism with regard to family life, education, recreation and labor. The city is a Communist utopia, built so from the ground up.

Because of the significance attached by the Soviets to their first brandnew socialistic city, neither money nor thought has been spared. Leading professors of economics and sociology were invited to contribute their ideas. Six of the foremost architectural societies and institutions in Russia submitted plans in a competition which was finally won by the High Technical School.

The challenge was one to stir the enthusiasm of any architect or engineer. The city was planned as a complete industrial unit. An automobile plant to be built near by was to employ 18,000 workers, one third of whom would be women. Six thousand additional women would be employed in the kitchen factory, bread factory, clubhouse and similar institutions. An allowance of 25 per cent was made for dependents, minors and other non-producers, making a total of 30,000 people. A steel plant not yet started was to employ an equal number of workers, bringing the total population, when everything was completed, to 60,000.

The High Technical Commission laid down the fundamental requirements of size, area per person, and the number and kind of functions to be provided for in the city. It then turned to American architects and engineers to "rationalize" the project, to use the parlance of the moment in Russia. Of this process of "rationalization" nothing has been more striking than the improvements made to the water, plumbing, heating and lighting systems.

The chief problem which confronted the designers was the proper density of population. Overcrowding is still one of the major concerns in the older and larger cities of Russia. Quite probably most of the Soviet officials interested in the development were only too familiar with the stuffy rooms, dark hallways and inadequate sanitation arrangements of the older communities. They desired for the new city abundant sunshine, fresh air and ample modern conveniences. Throughout the planning there was a conscious effort to raise the standard of living for the working people to a new level.

For social and practical reasons it was decided to divide the housing facilities into units for 1,000 persons each. Elevators were ruled out, both because of the extra expense and because of the frankly acknowledged fact that the Russian people are still distrustful of such contrivances. The housing units therefore took the form of five houses each, each house four stories high, connected with the other buildings of the unit by enclosed passages and accommodating 200 persons. In addition each "community unit" includes a clubhouse, a nursery building and a kindergarten building.

About ten acres of ground is allotted to each unit. Of this a little less than two acres is building area, the remaining eight acres being permanently reserved for lawns, walks, playgrounds and park space. One can picture the benefits to any large American city which this breathing space would give. No longer would there be the rush to the country on Sunday, or children growing up in ignorance of flowers and tadpoles and grasshoppers. The Soviet's attention to youth is practical and significant.

The life in any one community unit will be very much like that in any other. The clubhouse is its most significant feature and is really the nerve center of the group. In this building, 300 feet long and two stories high, provision is made for all social, educational, recreational and gastronomic needs of the adult population. Directly off the lobby into which one enters is a large dining hall which will accommodate one-third of the population of the unit at one time. There is also an open-air dining balcony for use during the Summer months. The club kitchens are on the order of serving pantries, since most of the food for the entire city is prepared in the central kitchen factory and sent out in a cooked or semi-prepared condition. As there are no regular kitchen facilities in the community houses, the club's kitchens supply every one, including those who for one reason or another do not use the club dining room.

Next in importance to the dining room is the auditorium, which serves also for a gymnasium and motion-picture theater. Adjoining it on the first floor are locker and shower rooms for men and women, and above these are the projection and film-storage rooms. In the hands of the Soviets the movie is a most important branch of education, instructing even those who cannot read. Even the posters, signs and graphs are so well adapted to the still widespread illiteracy that we foreigners, illiterate in Russian, can grasp their meaning as well as though they were printed in English.

The club buildings also contain a library, reading room, chess room, game room, telephone and telegraph room, notion shop, a political science study room, a laboratory for inventive experiments, and a room for the study of military science. They seem to justify, from the Soviet point of view, the title of "headquarters of civilization" which a young "consomol" [Komsomol, member of the Communist Youth League] bestowed upon a club building of similar type in a near-by town.

The club is not a school in the ordinary sense, but facilities for the stimulation and molding of adult minds are so conveniently provided that communism can hardly help taking root. The science laboratory is particularly noteworthy. There is a well-developed policy in the Soviet Government to encourage individual initiative along scientific and engineering lines, so that Russia will not have to depend upon foreign specialists.

So many functions are concentrated in the clubhouse that the only remaining use for the five community houses in the unit is as dormitories. These buildings are about 40 feet wide, 200 feet long and four stories high, and are constructed with brick side walls and concrete frame. The windows are double, as is necessary in the severe winters of this latitude, but are larger than the ordinary Russian window. The walls are insulated against the cold with a composition of wood chips and shavings, cemented in by an impregnating compound which makes the whole virtually fireproof, and floors and walls are soundproofed, so that the occupants may live with as little interference from one another as possible.

The first three floors are arranged alike, with single and double rooms alternating. Nine square meters (96.87 square feet) was fixed by the High Technical Schools Commission as the allowance for each person, and the sleeping rooms are all too small to permit any other uses than that for which they are designed. This limited amount of privacy is all that is permitted to the worker under the new scheme of living. Each room has a wardrobe and wash-basin, and each floor has a central lobby or lounging room and hot-plates for a limited amount of light cooking. The fourth floor of each building is composed of larger rooms, the size of a double and single room combined. These are intended to be occupied by "Communes"—groups of three or four young men or women who work, study and live together. Nobody worries about any moral questions that may arise from housing groups of both sexes on the same floor. So far as I know, there is no chaperonage of any kind, nor any restrictions covering the assignment of rooms. Beyond this fact we can only conjecture. We do find a good many young people who have been married twice or even three times before they are 30. On the subject of morals in general there is just as much dissension and divergence of opinion here among the Russians as there is over "prohibition" [of alcohol] at home. There are those who believe in the freedom the present law allows them and those who do not.

The nursery and kindergarten buildings are an integral part of each complete unit. The nursery is designed for children from 3 months to 3 or 4 years of age, of whom it is estimated that there will be about eighty-five in each unit. The building is planned to be an actual, full-time home for these children, with eating and sleeping quarters, and a staff of child specialists and nurses in charge. The degree of separation between children and parents will be largely a matter of choice on the part of the parents.

Many fathers and mothers, I believe, will be quite satisfied to have the government take over in large measure the care of their children. This would apply especially to the younger couples when both parents are working in the plant. Another inducement is that the nursery can often provide better or more suitable foods than the individual families are able to procure. For example, hospitals and nurseries share the limited supply of fine white flour and always receive preference in case of a shortage of milk. By many such indirect ways are the objects of the Soviets attained.

The kindergarten is planned for children between 4 and 7 years of age. Here emphasis is laid on project work, as it is in our own progressive schools; a woodworking shop is one of the principal features. Children are taken to visit factories where the Communist system may be seen at work, or to inspect some great construction project. I have seen dozens of groups of youngsters with their teachers visiting the site of the new town and being told of the important differences such enterprises will make in their own lives. The slogan, "the Five-Year Plan in four years," is everywhere.

The new city will not be limited to the units I have described. The new scheme of life is frankly admitted by the Soviets to be experimental. While its practicability is being demonstrated, workers who so desire will be allowed to live in apartment houses, identical in size and capacity with the community houses, but divided into apartments of three rooms with kitchen and bath. Each room is large, containing about twenty square meters. But unlike American practice, each family has one room rather than one apartment, and each kitchen has to serve for three families. This is not an innovation but is the plan generally followed in the cities at the present time.

In these apartment groups the clubhouses and school buildings are left unbuilt. The Soviet sociologists are not interested in putting more of their government's money into clubs, nurseries and kindergartens than is necessary to prove the correctness of their ideas. The city at first will be two-thirds apartment construction and one-third community units. But as soon as the practicability of the community unit plan has been demonstrated, the apartment houses can be transformed into units by adding partitions and erecting the club and school buildings.

Allan Austin and his associates would not remain in the Soviet Union long enough to learn that, in fact, apartment use was to evolve in a direction opposite to that which the communists had anticipated. The communal living units that Allan depicted with such empathy were not, in fact, popular among families. Most of those assigned to these units persisted in traditional patterns of family life despite the communal facilities provided. Indeed, some of the scheduled communal facilities were never completed. In 1930 the Soviets first "All-Union Congress of Human Behavior" had insisted upon the possibility of "a socially *open* man, who is easily collectivized, and quickly and profoundly transformed in his behavior."[5] However, human nature and human culture proved to be more stubborn.

It was on the construction site that Allan Austin had his own experiences with human nature.

May 21, 1930

The work on the City is getting an indifferent start, with considerable misdirected effort and general confusion about how it should be done—especially Metallostroy's indifferent way of carrying out our orders. We have just about succeeded in establishing ourselves as boss, but the results are not yet apparent. Tomorrow we will lay stone in the foundations, but much temporary construction is still undone. Autostroy is giving us full support and putting the responsibility squarely up to us to get things done; then they back us up on our demands to Metallostroy. I believe that we will soon be on a working basis where things will begin to click. Anyway it is very interesting work, and taxes one's ingenuity to do what we want to do with as little equipment and skilled labor available as we have.

Yesterday afternoon I was over at the Industrial Plant with Appleton, looking at some foundations being laid. The masonry work was ragged and sloppy. So App complained to the foreman about it and was told that the masons were apprentices, and that this was the first day they had ever worked. They were young boys and girls, just about high school age, and fresh from the city. There had not been sufficient instructors to give them help and they had gotten along as best they could. They were all sunburned and fiery red, yet interested to know how they had done.

It was hard to criticize their work for they had tried hard. There are a good many girl bricklayers too, though I have not seen any of their work. I intend to take one reel of movies illustrating women's work on this job. It includes almost everything. One house has been entirely stuccoed by girls who are learning the trade.

It is possible that Allan was experiencing the results of conflict between Autostroy and Metallostroy. The Soviet engineering group supported Austin Company field management, but the labor organization was still searching for a communist approach to the mobilization of construction workers.

May 24, 1930

The job is trying our patience a good deal these days, for the Russian temperament is lots different from the American, and their labor organization such that there is no flexibility to the work the men are doing. Russians make promises recklessly, and usually forget about them. They love nothing better than an argument or discussion and will drop everything to get in on a conference. They are among the world's greatest talkers and get correspondingly little done.

The men work mostly on piecework, even in many cases where it would seem impossible to us; and consequently you cannot change a man from one job to another until he is finished with the first. He usually works all day on one item. If I want a few men to move some lumber, they must send to the office and get men especially for that purpose. We are not yet completely organized in the field, and perhaps some of these conditions can be bettered as time goes on, but now at the start it is the dickens of a job to get anything done as you want it. If there is a wrong way it seems as though they will invariably take it. And it is also obvious that Metallostroy and ourselves are working to cross-purposes much of the time, and that situation must be adjusted soon.

May 26, 1930

The present situation is rather highly charged with disgust and ragged nerves from the contrariness, both intentional and unintentional, of the Metallostroy gang. They seem to be knifing us in the back at every opportunity, and that is the hardest thing for me to stand without losing my temper. We expect, and find, general inefficiency and ignorance of modern methods, and lack of all kinds of tools and equipment; but then they deliberately work contrary to our orders, and fail to make the best use of what facilities they do have, it is mighty hard to be amiable and keep from getting cross with them. The effort to control my temper takes more effort than anything else I do.

6

"THE FIRST HOME WE HAVE HAD"

May 19, 1930

Dearest Mother and Dad—

They are now at work plastering the exterior of our houses. This work was delayed until now to avoid possibility of frost. Several houses are practically complete, and the improvement in appearance is considerable. When they have painted the wood trim they should look very presentable and not the least temporary. We are still shy on a number of necessary articles of furniture, notably wicker chairs, as we have only straight-backed chairs now. But the place is seeming quite like home and is very comfortable. We also lack shades of any kind and screens, which are becoming quite necessary. Also linoleum.

I can record today the passing of the last visible bit of snow on the hills opposite. We are having fine, warm days now with bright sunshine. I got quite burned in the field today. But the weather is variable. Very little rain has fallen to date but we can expect some next month, I believe.

News had reached Cleveland that some wives were discouraged by their circumstances. So Allan's mother Ida had written a letter to cheer Margretta.

After reading Mother's letter, Margretta said to tell her that she was not at all downhearted and to rest easy on that point. There are several women who need bolstering up quite a lot. Mrs. S in particular is a wet blanket to the whole party and can find nothing good about the country or her situation here. [She was the wife of Allan's immediate superior.] Just a few dissenters can do a lot of damage in a place like this where everyone is thrown so close together and there are no secrets, so to speak.

Mother asked about the difference in time. We are eight hours from Cleveland here, and so Margretta is eleven hours from her family [in California]. That gives as good an idea of the distance as anything.

... May 21

Today was rest day for most of the men but several, including myself, stayed at work as we cannot all leave at the same time. Margretta went into Nijni and got her hair cut, a fairly good job. She bought a large Paisley shawl to cover the trunk in our living room, and a very interesting little icon. We have a number of these now. They are not difficult to get but, of course, very old ones in good condition are rare. So our apartment is acquiring a more furnished and native atmosphere.

Allan's letter grew long, as the departure of an Austin employee, who would carry it to Cleveland, was delayed. With that employee Allan planned to send movie film portraying the construction work to date.

... May 24

This is getting more like a diary than a letter but I shall keep on till Bob leaves. Fixing up the Club House has occupied the attention of Margretta and Mrs. Davis for the last day or two. They were in Nijni today getting some furnishings, paints, *objects d'art,* etc.

Margretta also got several additions to our collection of ornaments: a very fine large china plate, an old copper tea kettle to hang on the andirons, and a bust of Lenin. It is almost obligatory to have a picture or bust of him displayed. You must learn to pronounce his name Lêyn-yin.

On the back of this photo of her living room Margretta wrote, "The fluff in the middle of our oriental rug is Romeo, the cat, washing himself. Icons, and a bust of Lenin, are in the mantel recess." Margretta appreciated icons as religious art, but, as a Methodist, she did not use them for devotions. Lenin was present as a courtesy to their hosts. *Margretta Austin, Russia Album*

This evening we had our first cucumbers. They are very tender and nicely flavored. Butter has just gone to 8 rubles 25 kopecks per kilo, or about $1.90 per pound. It jumped from 4 rubles overnight, and it isn't much good at that—quite greasy and pale. Eggs about 7½¢ each. I imagine that the summer and fall will bring a considerably larger variety of vegetables and fruits, but I shudder for next winter. . . .

. . . May 26

I am in the midst of a job of interior decorating, the conception and execution of which is unique in the records of that industry, I believe. Wait 'till you come, and I'll show you something different, at least. . . .

Today the Ford sedan which Appleton will use arrived in good shape and was immediately put to work. It was in good shape till Mr. Bryant slammed the door and broke the glass first thing. Mr. Miter's Buick ought to be along any day, and we have some hope of getting the various boxes of phonographs, movie, stationery, etc. which were shipped at the same time. . . .

Although Allan was the most junior of the Austin team, he had—as the son of the company president—certain diplomatic duties to perform.

Tomorrow night we are entertaining Mr. and Mrs. Makarovsky at dinner, with an interpreter also. It is the first of any "official" entertaining that I know of and in line with what we agreed was a good thing for us to do here. We shall borrow a Victrola and use music for the *piece de resistance,* as far as entertaining goes. It needs less interpretation. The present limited choice of food at the store makes a fancy menu impossible, but Margretta will concoct something good and different for them. Croquettes are about the fanciest dish we can make from meat, for then it is ground enough to taste tender and can be diluted and disguised with other things.

. . . May 30th.

Well, we had our dinner last night, but as usual in Russia things didn't turn out just as planned. The guests were an hour and a quarter late. After waiting an hour, Margretta and I started to eat. When we were half way through the company arrived. Before we opened the door we made a record clearing of the table. When they came in, Margretta served a dinner that to all appearances was on schedule and perfectly O.K. But it was a job to keep up the illusion. Fortunately we hadn't gotten to the lemon pie yet, and that made quite an impression.

The evening was enjoyable and gay. Though we had an interpreter, there was much direct conversation back and forth, exchanging words as it were. Mr. Makarovsky speaks some English and is teaching his wife. Mrs. Makarovsky is a former opera singer, and as we had borrowed a Victrola for the occasion we could entertain her nicely with our collection of Carouso, Galli-Curci, and others. She was quite appreciative. From her stage career she has kept bright spots: notably her eyes, lips, and fingernails. So the evening turned out all right.

. . . May 30th.

Last night there was a dinner at the Club House for everyone, and I think 38 were present. The cook there is fairly good, in a Russian style. We had goose.

Today we're all going on a picnic on the Volga on a chartered boat. It promises to be a great treat, for most of us have not been very far away since we came here.

Allan

Allan appended to the letter a "List for the Russian Refugees," things he wished his parents to bring on their visit planned for August: blankets, mosquito bite dope, ant powder, fly swatters, oral and cooking thermometers, furniture stain and brushes, tools, a flashlight, an electric hot plate. The latter "will be extremely useful as it will enable Margretta to cook some things without being over the hot wood stove." He also specified a book of Russian language lessons and "a book written by, or explaining, Karl Marx's theories."

Then Margretta typed her own list; it included baking powder, Crisco, vinegar, spices, canning supplies, "canned goods of any kind would be heavenly," cosmetics, underwear, and stockings. Apparently she had hired a young women to help with housework, for she requested inexpensive silk material "for Thelma [possibly an interpreter] and my maids":

They love the silk we have so much and they can't buy it, so we promised them that in August they would each have some. This is important, as their little hearts are set on it. . . .

I will need several more knitted suits for winter; I haven't nearly enough, as I found out. Though not expensive, they should be nice looking. Even here we dress up and try to look our best. I always change for dinner in the evening. I think the Russians are disappointed that we do not fix up even more. . . .

Upon more thought and discussion we have decided that you need not bring me winter apparel. I will have to go to Germany to get fitted up before the winter begins, principally because I will need a winter fur coat. Strange as it may seem there are no decent furs in Russia.

Construction of the housing complex had begun a fortnight after the ceremonial groundbreaking at the factory site. In his next letter Allan was able to report meaningful progress during the first twelve days of this work, despite a crippling lack of electricity and of site drainage.

June 1, 1930

Dear Dad—

I shall describe the condition of the Workers City on this date. Ground was broken 12 days ago (May 18).

Lines and grades are established for the fifteen buildings on the south side of Unit No. 1, and this work is proceeding on the other fifteen buildings on the north side. We have the following facilities for the first fifteen buildings: Standard gauge track in and operating; narrow gauge from brick storage piles to serve five buildings. Water pipe is installed and pumping from one well, with occasional failure of the pump, which is being operated by a tractor. A second well is being tied into the system and will afford greater volume and constancy. Four material sheds, 12 x 24 meters, are built to supply the first 10 buildings; they are partially stocked with cement and tools. Two mortar mixers and three cement mixers, some lacking their electric motors, are on site. We lack electric power, which should have been installed by this time. The main drainage ditch, over 1900 meters long, is 75% complete, but actual drainage of the site into this ditch is not begun.

The first four buildings, Nos. 10, 9, 8, 7, are completely excavated. Rubble stone foundations and piers are 80% complete in 10 and 9; 40% in 8. No brickwork or floor construction is started. Nor are any lintels cast. We plan to pre-cast all the concrete lintels, about 5,000 in all. To start with, it will be necessary to wash our gravel by hand here on the job until the washing plant at the dock is in operation.

There are approximately 750 men (and women) engaged on this department of the job at present. The number is increasing daily. There have been several important changes in Metallostroy's organization on the job; I feel that we are in better shape to proceed effectively with the work. Just today we succeeded in getting from them an organization chart, based on our recommendations, that establishes definite responsibility for each part of the work. This will help us a lot. Sprackling [superintendent of the Worker's City project] and I have divided our work: he is looking after all drawings and their interpretation, and the quality and correctness of workmanship on the job. I lay out temporary construction, do job organization, schedule the operations, place (or try to) men and materials to the best advantage.

 Allan

Then the temperature plunged, and morale plunged with it.

June 4, 1930

Dear Mother and Dad—

We are concerned about the food situation due to freakish weather. The temperature dropped below freezing for several nights. You know what that would do to the fruit crop, and to vegetables also. The stores and markets have even fewer things. We have had no fruit for two weeks, except dried figs, and they are poor. Prunes, our mainstay, have now given out, as have apples. Cucumbers are coming in and that is a help. It may soon be advisable to try to bring in food from Berlin, but of course that would be difficult and expensive.

It seems foolish to complain, for there just isn't any relief possible. But every now and then I get fed up with the whole situation and wonder why I came. Absolutely nothing seems to go off as planned. A sense of humor is necessary, but it doesn't help all the time.

Tomorrow is a rest day and I'll celebrate it by going to Nijni for my monthly haircut. Thus we pass the time with simple things. It will be a wonderful experience *when it is over.* The gang as a whole is getting along well, with a few notable exceptions.

Allan

Margretta stepped in to bolster team morale with a humorous newsletter, typed in two columns, for posting in the "Club House," a common facility that the twenty-some Austin Company engineers, including five families, shared. The masthead announced "THE WEEKLY WAIL" from "Austingrad, U.S.S.R., June 7, 1930." In the upper right-hand corner was the "*Weather forecast:* By official decree, summer has been struck off this year's calendar." Among a dozen gossipy paragraphs was a report that "the ladies are all excited this week by the absence of butter and the addition of lettuce to the menu. It is most touching to see their faces light up when a green vegetable comes into view. Of course the men are not interested. One of the reporters tells me, though, of one husband who bodily carried his wife over to the store to be sure she bought him some lettuce."

Allan's spirits recovered with the weather. He and Margretta requested token gift items to smooth some work relationships:

June 7, 1930

Dear Dad and Mother—

Our summer has nearly returned now and it feels a lot better, after June snow storms. Day before yesterday we went into Nijni on the boat and had a nice, leisurely day wandering around and eating lunch in the park. The government-operated antique store has a constantly changing stock of fine things taken from former estates so there is always the chance of getting something unusual. We bought several interesting things which we'll show you when you come. . . .

Can Margaret [Allan's sister] get us about three or four dollars worth of 10¢ jewelry, or 25¢, mostly ear rings, which are very popular? Also, if you can buy a couple of cigarette lighters for a dollar or less, I could give them away very effectively. I would also like half a dozen cheap automatic pencils, such as they have in a 25¢ store, in red or green finish, and gold-filled trimmings. They can't be too fancy to suit the Russians. . . .

Work on the City is proceeding slowly, for we are still hampered by lack of facilities, changes in drawings, and now by a shortage of men. We have approximately 1,100 on the job. . . .

Mr. Miter's Buick came today and is a very swell car; by far the most luxurious ever seen in these parts.

Goodbye,
    Allan

June 15, 1930

Dear Families—

Today is both Sunday and a rest day. We celebrated the occasion with a short religious service this morning in the Club House. Margretta was instrumental in arranging it and the support and attendance were gratifying. About 25 were there. Mr. Miter, once a Sunday School Superintendent, conducted it. The result was very pleasing. . . .

Recently we have all been depressed over working conditions here, but at the moment I feel better and we may soon see improvements sufficient to bolster our spirits. As Bill Wolfe said, "If there weren't any difficulties, we wouldn't be needed here." So our job is principally overcoming difficulties, which is enough. . . .

    Allan

June 18, 1930

Dearest Mother, Dad, Margaret and Don—

. . . You were asking about the initials C.C.A. which we put at the top of our letters. That is the Russian equivalent of U.S.A. They put the address upside down from our way of writing it, so C.C.A. at the top gives the Russian post office the initials of our country in their own language. Then

Mother asked whether the initials U.S.S.R. were sufficient, instead of writing Russia. This is, in fact, more correct. It stands for Union of Soviet Socialist Republics. And these initials in Russian become C.C.C.P.

This morning Mrs. Bryant and her sister arrived with Mr. Bryant. Margretta is having tea for the two ladies tomorrow afternoon.

I must tell you of our experience last night. A theatrical company from Moscow has been playing in Nijni for several days, so I got eight tickets. The Davises, Makarovskys and Colemans went with us, in the Buick. I had understood that the operetta was "Rosalie," but it turned out to be "Rose-Marie," the good old U.S. story, music, etc. It was interesting and often amusing to see the Russian representation of Canadian scenery and atmosphere. The Indians were simply terrifying. Costuming and scenery revealed the limited resources here, but the voices and acting were quite good. With long intermissions it was one o'clock before we left the theater.

Home and to bed was uppermost in our minds. But as we drove across the pontoon bridge our lights showed something strange ahead. Bless us, the bridge was open, two pontoons out. Each night they do that [to let Oka river traffic pass]. We knew that perfectly well, but didn't expect to be so late.

We were fortunate to have Mr. Makarovsky with us. We returned to Autostroy's main office in Nijni where he telephoned and found that there were no rooms to be had in any hotels. After their previous experiences at the Russia Hotel, the women much preferred to stay right in the car. There are sleeping quarters for various officials in Autostroy's office, so Mr. Makarovsky got one large room with four beds in it. The women were firm in their desire to stay in the car, so we locked it—and, by the way, the policeman on the beat, and four others nearby, were all *women*. So they had a real feminine guard. We took the beds, and slept for about 2½ hours. When Mr. Makarovsky woke us at 4:30 it was broad daylight, of course. We went down to find all the ladies still asleep. We waited at the bridge till 5:30 when it was finally put together again. It was a rather interesting operation to watch. . . .

On the bottom of my left foot I have some sort of scaly infection, so this morning I went over to the job hospital to have the doctor look at

The Austin family and employees picnicked in the Russian countryside. Wilbert, wearing a light-colored hat, is seated on the bench, and Ida sits next to him. Directly in front of them is their daughter Margaret. Margretta, who wore a fur-trimmed coat to this picnic, wrote on the back of the photo, "All looking very handsome with our mouths full!"
Margretta Austin Christmas Album

it. Don't concern yourselves, for the medical attention here is very good. Their little hospital is quite complete and the doctor high-grade....

    Allan

On June 23 George Bryant took his family to Moscow for a month of negotiations over contract disputes that will be described in the next chapter. Edith Bryant and her sister, Alice Hadrgon, were timid about venturing from their hotel during the long days when Bryant was occupied with business. On July 14 Margretta Austin joined them. According to a Bryant biographer, "After 'Mrs. A' arrived, the ladies seemed to go for more walks, shopped more often and frequently bought fruits such as strawberries, cherries and apricots in the open markets."[1]

Margretta continued with the Bryants to Southhampton, England, where they met Wilbert and Ida Austin, along with their second son Donald and their daughter Margaret, on July 23. There is a three-month break in Allan's letters while his family was traveling. The Austin party arrived in Nizhny

In a Nizhny Novgorod photo studio Margretta took steps to get a smile from Allan. This is a page from an album she mailed to her mother and her brothers in time for Christmas 1930. *Margretta Austin Christmas Album*

Novgorod during a period when both the Austin Company and Autostroy were evaluating whether the vast construction project could continue.

In June and July Margretta had risen to the task of bolstering the morale of the Austin Company engineers, their resident families, and the visiting Bryant family. However, by the time she returned to Russia, she needed a boost herself. Yet she had now to play hostess to Allan's parents, brother and sister. Usually she relished such a role, but emotional fatigue plus a slight injury dampened her enthusiasm. Months later she apologized to her mother-in-law, Ida: "I didn't do all that I should have last summer, or all that I wanted to, and can only lay it to my foot not being well, for I know that my spirit was willing. Give me another chance and I will try to make you very happy."

Nevertheless, Allan's first letter after his parents' visit glowed with appreciation. Their presence and assistance helped Allan to feel that the Russian apartment that he and Margretta shared had become, truly, their "first home."

September 26, 1930

Dearest Mother and Dad—

The foliage is turning quite rapidly now and soon we will have all the fall colors. About a week ago we celebrated Margretta's birthday with a party at our house for the four families in the apartment.

We have managed to install several improvements in our apartment: breadbox, fire screen, curtain rods with curtains hung upon them, and last night I varnished the dining table. The fire screen I designed is not bad for a first attempt. It has the classic simplicity of Early American wrought iron and, better still, it cost nothing.

With the substantial improvements which you furnished us, we are getting quite homey. Both of us appreciate your generosity to us in contributing things and transporting other items we needed so much. It adds a whole lot to the life here to know that you are both able and willing to help us when we need it.

We enjoyed your visit and were pleased to have you in our home. It is the first home we have had—different from the usual—but none the less our home. You were our first visitors, which seems right and proper. I enjoyed it particularly on that account and I have much to remember from your visit.

7

"OFF THE ROAD"

By midsummer 1930, it was apparent that work on the giant project was not proceeding well. The problems that Allan Austin noted at the Worker's City site were compounded at the larger and more complex factory construction site. Boris Agapov, a Russian reporter sent to Nizhny Novgorod in July, wrote that a great vision was being strangled by confusion. In an article published in the Soviet newspaper *For Industrialization* under the title "Off the Road," Agapov imaged the vast project as a Russian-made rattle-trap car, ready to tip over.[1]

The [Metallostroy] Chief of Construction is driving. The machine creeks and shakes, everything rattling down to the last screw. It drops into un-expected ruts, turns around holes in the road, maneuvering, slowing down and then putting on speed. One false turn of the wheel, one un-noticed rut, and it may turn over. Suddenly a stop. Catastrophe? No, it is the Office.

   We get out of the "Ford." I sit down in the corner. I shall not disturb anybody, but observe how the heart of the construction job is working—

On July 31, 1930, Russian workers poured cement from a Model AA dump truck for the first concrete road outside a major Soviet city. At left The Austin Company supervisor for factory construction, Walter Baggaley, stands watchfully above the wet slurry, ready with a finishing trowel. *GAZ Museum of History*

the center from which many "wires" go to all future buildings, shops, schools, roads, garages, kitchen, factories, community houses. There are wooden walls where the dusty sun is playing. There are drawings and schedules all over the table.

One schedule shows the progress of work through the 20th of July. In the Forge Shop, instead of 14% only 7% has been done. Spring Shop, instead of 11%—5%. Machine and Maintenance, instead of 90%—45%. Employment Office, instead of 50%, only 23%.

The Chief is speaking by telephone about food for workers. He is only 3 weeks at the job. He must put right what was spoiled by others. Who is guilty that only half of the schedule has been carried out?

On the walls are plans. One is written in Russian and in English, "General Plan of Autoplant at Monostyrka." Through the white lines on this blueprint I can see the future plant. I see the concrete road, first in the USSR. It is smooth like the enamel on an automobile and straight like the ray of a searchlight. Fourteen thousand vehicles are moving along it, four in a row. They come from the Assembly Shop, the biggest shop in Europe, one-and-a-half kilometers long.

The Pressed Steel Building, Spring Shop, Forge Shop, Pumping Stations, Storage Buildings, Garages, Woodworking Shop, Electric Station, Tool and Die Forge Shop, are planned in rows, collecting and reflecting the sun's rays in their glass walls. Behind them, among forests and parks, is the New City [a pun—*novyi gorod* means "new city"]—the City of Socialism. Streets divide it into rectangles where, like flowers in a bed, there is housing among the trees. Every rectangle of housing includes a Club House, Nurseries and Kindergarten, Dining Halls, Libraries, Bathtubs and Showers working day and night. On the edge of the city are playing fields and green parks. Its sky is not spoiled by soot or smoke. It is a city without chimneys and stoves, lighted by electricity and heated by steam.

I do not know how its 50,000 people will look, what music will sound in its gardens, or what will be discussed in the meetings of its Executive Committees. I know only that it will appear as a leap into the future, that the City and the Plant will change life, that these white lines on the blueprint mean not only walls of new buildings but new ways, unseen in human life until now.

What I see is enough to call this a City of Dreams, Utopia, "Bolsheviks' Nonsense." Yet an exact drawing of these ravings is on the table of the Chief Manager of the Construction. The first floors of the Utopia are ready, the white bricks are glittering, and millions of rubles are allocated. The town *shall* be. One of the greatest factories in Europe shall also be. Thousands of people will live and work here in spite of the present road sign, "No Thoroughfare"—in spite of the fact that vehicles now creak and shake on this road.

One day when we look out over the factory and the city we will remember the past blindness, the quarrels between engineers, the wooden

barracks, the tired workers, the lack of materials, the failures, the delays, and the moments of despair. We shall remember it as people remember a sad childhood, or the years of study and cruel war, out of which they have emerged victors. But now . . .

Now the door opens and the equipment operators come in, people sent here by the Moscow Department of Metallostroy. They are the screws in the vehicle that the Manager is driving. They are the strongest men in Nizhny. They can, during one hour, dig a ditch that fifty men could not excavate. During 24 hours, only by pressing the handle of the elevator, they can unload as much sand as 600 persons, working three shifts, could do. They can wash as much gravel for concrete as 1,000 men. On the skill with which they guide the iron power of their elevators, cranes, and concrete mixers will depend the speed, quality, and cost of construction. I dare not speak to such athletes. I shall write them a letter:

"Highly esteemed managers and engineers of Metallostroy, and respected Moscow Directors: Do you know that the plant must be built in fifteen months? Do you know that to achieve such speed workers must be assisted by machines? Do you know that there is a lack of labor, a deficit of 3,000 people? It is difficult to overcome this deficit because the officials in charge of labor distribution are not allowed to recruit workers from anywhere except the Nizhny Novgorod district. In addition, some workers must leave the job at harvest time.

"You arranged the delivery of gravel which is the foundation of all construction. You sent a dredge and a gravel washer. The gravel washer was old and badly repaired. You hung it on brackets. When the old thing was fired up it shook, coughed, choked, and died. You [Soviet engineers] who receive big salaries spat into the river, looked at the broken machine, and watched local workers load gravel with shovels. You knew that the construction needed ten times more gravel than these workers could supply. Yet you sat there from June 8th to July 16th until the new Manager of Construction, Mr. Tsarevsky, arrived. He sent your "mechanization" to the devil, and placed a simple sieve under the dredge because there was nothing else to do.

"Now we are on the dock. There are 15,000 tons of gravel. There are pyramids of sand. Here comes rubble stone, cement, machines, lumber.

Opposite: Under construction in August 1930 were the Woodworking Shop (*above*) and the second-floor slab of the Pressed Steel Building (*below*). Note the three temporary railways used to deliver cement for pouring and (*at right*) the boom of an American crawler crane used to hoist materials. *The Austin Company Archives*

Buildings cry for all this. Do you have a plan for their delivery? Every day dock workers receive new instructions from you. Every day you make people destroy and re-make what was done yesterday. Summer days pass and you sigh softly while young Communists (*Komsomols*) from all districts carry gravel on their shoulders while the movable conveyors rust in storage. An unfortunate pump is carried from place to place because you cannot indicate its proper place. The expensive North-West crane, which could replace 200 workers, stands unassembled on the dock because nobody guarded its motor when the crane was delivered.

"Your storage looks like piles of scrap-iron, although it includes parts of valuable foreign machines.

"Visit the different districts for the first time in your life—you have never been there! Don't be afraid to spoil your shoes. Here was your conflict with the Americans who demanded to dismantle one section of roof because the concrete, mixed by hand, was rotten. A quarter kilometer distant, a ready concrete mixer had been standing for three months waiting . . . for what? For you to be honest!"

What has the Workers' Committee done to mobilize the workers' groups? It did not call a single workers' meeting in the districts to discuss the reasons for delay and how to avoid delay. It did not organize anything. Cultural work? No. There was no cultural work at the job where 8,000 are working. A splendid Club House is standing empty. There are not even movies because the technicians do not know how to install the film projector.

The Workers' Committee does not know how many shock brigades— groups of social competition—there are or how they worked. It is enough to say that once there were 75 shock brigades but the Committee could not keep up with them. The number of shock brigades in July was 27. Such is the Workers' Committee.

While you are riding a vehicle with loose screws, you think about ways to repair the vehicle. First you must fix the motor. Then throw away unnecessary ballast—not in Nizhny but in Moscow where they make the leaden stuff. The new Manager of Construction cannot drive if the wheel is broken. When the unnecessary ballast is thrown away, then we shall look at a clean job. We will see how people struggle for their future.

НЕ ПОДНИМАЙСЯ НА НЕИСПЫТАННОМ КАНАТЕ

There were other demoralizing problems. The Austin Company did not believe that it was being paid properly. The contract with Autostroy stipulated that Austin would be paid for construction supervision on a monthly basis, "at the rate of four percent of the actual cost of these works," including "the cost of construction materials" and "the wages of workers." Austin interpreted this as the cost of construction materials brought to the site, while Autostroy wished to tie the fee to materials actually incorporated into construction each month. Metallostroy's inability to organize labor and machinery efficiently meant that materials were piling up, yet only half the scheduled work was being accomplished—despite the best efforts of Austin Company supervisors.

On projects in the United States it had been possible to link supervision payments to the cost of labor. The Austin Company and American labor unions had similar understandings of work rules, and the company itself paid the workers at the end of each week. Here there was no agreement on work rules, Metallostroy paid the workers, and the Austin Company was in the dark. On June 8, 1930, Harry Miter complained to Autostroy about its calculations upon which Austin's first monthly fee would be based.

> The preliminary estimate furnished us today amounts to 123,282 Rubles. The figures represent the approximate percentage of work completed [upon which a 4% payment to Austin would be calculated], but we did not agree to accept only the work performed at the plant and the Community Building as the basis of computation. We have been informed unofficially that an amount in excess of 5,000,000 Rubles have been expended to May 31, 1930. You will agree, we are sure, that the amount shown on your preliminary estimate for payment is but an infinitesimal portion of the total actually expended. . . .
>
> We are asking for nothing beyond that which our contract calls for. . . . It is needless to say that had conditions been at all favorable much more actual construction could have been performed.[2]

In other words, Autostroy was proposing to pay the Austin Company 4,931 rubles, or $2,542 at the agreed rate of exchange, for their first month's work on the job. The Austin Company claimed that it was owed at least 200,000 rubles, or $103,000, twenty-five times as much.

Payments to the Austin Company under the contract had to be made in dollars, and Autostroy may have felt the pinch of Russia's deepening foreign-exchange crisis. Later that fall, after the harvest season, the *Cleveland Press* carried an article that portrayed a deep crisis, Soviet denials, and American prejudices.[3]

Lack of Cash Forces Russia to Dump Goods

Foreign dispatches today told of another large shipment of wheat en route from Russia to Great Britain, presumably destined to be "dumped" in the world market.

At the same time, United Press wires carried the statement of Joseph V. Stalin, Communist leader, that reports of Soviet "dumping" were untrue.

The grain trade here understands that the Soviets are selling wheat regardless of cost. . . . Dispatches, denied by Soviet officials, report bread being rationed to the population while the government exports large quantities of wheat at prices below the cost of production. Cheap shipments of sugar, butter, [wood] pulp and other items have been reported. . . .

To pay for huge imports of machinery needed to carry out their industrialization program, the Soviets, it is presumed, have been forced to sacrifice products needed at home to raise the cash. . . .

The United States has little to fear from the alleged "dumping." Russia's share of the total world export trade is only slightly more than 1 per cent, as contrasted with 4 per cent before the World War. Half the exports are of oil and lumber.

Soviet exports had fallen because of difficulties with collectivization. Despite Stalin's denials, it was true that food needed to provide an adequate diet to the Russian people was being sold on the world market to secure foreign exchange for industrialization. However, it was unfair to single out the Soviets for "dumping" goods onto a market where prices often fell below the cost of production. During the Great Depression every nation was doing the same thing. The Soviet contribution to depressing world commodity prices was miniscule. It would be several years before America's new president, Franklin Roosevelt, implemented a controversial but imaginative plan to burn surplus crops in the field in an effort to stabilize commodity prices.

The same article noted that "Amtorg Trading Company today reported an order for 2200 knocked-down Ford trucks and passenger cars for shipment to

Nizhni-Novgorod." These vehicles would be assembled during 1931 on the temporary line set up in the old city.

The payment dispute with the Austin Company in June of 1930 led Autostroy to reopen contract negotiations in Moscow. Indeed, on the basis of an internal review of progress in Nizhni Novgorod, Autostroy prepared to cancel its contract with the Austin Company altogether. Autostroy was satisfied with Ford as a business partner but critical of Austin. To Autostroy investigators the Austin Company seemed incompetent in big construction works: it asked too many questions about what to do and how to do it; it showed lack of initiative and a need for guidance. Austin engineers rejected "subtle calculations aimed at the economy of materials," preferring familiar standards. Austin specialized in contracting where it was in full control, the report noted, but here it found itself caught between two rivals, Autostroy and Metallostroy. Soviet inexperience, Autostroy conceded, also contributed to Austin's apparent helplessness.[4]

Mr. P. Ya. Ziev, manager of Amtorg Trading Company and soon to be head of foreign relations for the All-Union Automobile and Tractor Association (VATO), told Harry Miter the news that Autostroy was considering a contract cancellation. In response to this surprising information, Miter prepared a thoughtful letter to Mr. Ziev, a letter in the "friendly spirit" that the contracting parties had promised to employ.

June 28th, 1930

. . . We are endeavoring to approach the discussion of this difficult situation in a broad, friendly spirit without resorting to any technical interpretation of the agreement . . . signed August 23rd, 1929, ten months ago. . . . A comparison of conditions then with the conditions now shows that many serious and important changes have occurred. The crash in the American Stock Market last fall has shaken the world and no one can estimate the damage done.

Many things have increased the problems of the [Soviet] Government. We want you to know we are endeavoring to consider the position of the Government in having to face these new problems.

Miter pointed out that the performance promised by the Austin Company in the contract was conditional upon efficient Soviet assistance. "When the agreement was being negotiated, The Austin Company said that if the Government would furnish the necessary American construction equipment, American fabricated steel, steel sash, and all other assistance needed in the way of labor and materials, then The Austin Company could complete the project by August 1st, 1931, and do it in accordance with its best American practice; this is the thought contained in the agreement." After a lengthy review of engineering disagreements and delays for which he believed Autostroy responsible, Miter emphasized that engineering delays had not affected the pace of construction. Progress was being retarded only by a scarcity of materials and a shortage of workers, for which the Soviets alone were responsible. "If every plan that could possibly be called for by the Agreement had been on the job May 1st, 1930, the work would not be one day further ahead. *There has been no delay* in the progress of the construction work due to lack of plans nor will it be possible to charge any delay in completion beyond August 1st, 1931, to lack of plans."[5]

Ziev of Amtorg apparently acted as intermediary between the Austin Company and Autostroy. He probably had further conversations with George Bryant, who gathered his family, which had been visiting Nizhny Novgorod, and sped to Moscow about this time. On July 1, Miter offered Ziev a compromise proposal: "On account of abnormal business conditions in the USSR at the present time, the cost of this plant may increase many times over what was contemplated. . . . We can arrive at an agreement with reference to limitation of our fee."[6]

This offer broke the log-jam. George Bryant negotiated a "Second Supplemental Agreement," which Autostroy and the Austin Company signed on July 18, 1930.[7] An entirely new payment scheme was set in place. The Austin Company would receive a total of $250,000 for its design and engineering work; of this, $200,000 had been paid already. The rest would be paid upon completion of design for the foundry, the building that Austin and Soviet engineers had argued about fiercely during the spring.

The time allowed for construction was extended three months, to December 1, 1931. For supervision of construction at Nizhny Novgorod, estimated to cost forty million dollars or more, Austin would now be paid a fixed fee of nine hundred thousand dollars—about 2%. This fee replaced all disputed calculations based upon the cost of labor and materials. Of this amount, $150,000 would be paid in Cleveland in four days, on July 22, 1930. This payment more than satisfied the earlier claims made by the Austin Company. Beginning on August 1, the Austin Company would receive regular monthly payments, beginning at forty thousand dollars and rising to fifty thousand, until payment was completed on December 1, 1931.

The total compensation that the Austin Company received for design of the factory and the Worker's City and for supervising their construction was $1,550,000. In more normal times, and on an American contract, the company would have expected to receive about four million dollars for designing and supervising a job of this magnitude. But times were not normal. On the one hand, the supervision required in Russia was far more demanding than in America. On the other hand, as the Great Depression deepened, the company had little American work in prospect. It was better to continue with a contract that would support the company, even if it would not enrich it. Beyond monetary concerns there was the challenge itself: the Austin Company had never retreated from a construction challenge, and it would not do so here.

In today's currency the revised Soviet contract was worth about seventeen million dollars to the company. The proceeds from this contract did in fact support the Austin Company, not only during the construction period but for several years thereafter.

Another part of the Second Supplemental Agreement relieved the Austin Company of responsibility for the design of the Power House and the supervision of its construction. Apparently Autostroy had found a European partner that could provide electrical generating equipment more cheaply or with more favorable terms of credit.

Autostroy also assumed direct responsibility for the design of support facilities for the Worker's City: "Bath, Laundry, Bread-Factory, Kitchen-Factory, School, Polyclinic, Department-Store, and the exterior lighting of Workers' City." Here too Autostroy hoped to utilize less expensive European or Soviet equipment. Austin, however, would review Autostroy's plans for these auxiliary facilities and would remain responsible for their construction.

Lines of authority were clarified. Autostroy reaffirmed its responsibility to make sure that Austin's instructions were executed. "The engineering and technical staff of The CONCERN [the Austin Company] supervising the construction work shall issue orders in the fields and give all information, during the progress of work, directly to the Field Superintendents of AUTOSTROY and other organizations engaged in the execution of the work. . . . All orders of the CONCERN relating to the supervision of construction and installation of equipment must be fully carried out by AUTOSTROY or its contractors."

Despite these strong words George Bryant, who negotiated for the Austin Company, remained skeptical that Autostroy and Metallostroy could in fact follow instructions and keep the work moving. Autostroy, in turn, remained skeptical of the Austin Company's ability to complete engineering and to supervise construction on this scale. The most striking provision of this new contract was one that provided for its cancellation. "Article 17. After 90 days from August 1, 1930, both parties have the right to cancel this Agreement with reference to construction supervision. Notice of cancellation to be given in writing in the first of the month and CONCERN's work is to cease two months from this date." If the Austin Company chose to cancel the contract, it would forfeit the forty-thousand-dollar fee for its final month of supervision. If Autostroy chose to cancel, it must pay supervision fees to the date of termination, plus a hundred thousand dollars.

In other words, the three and a half months from July 18 through October 31 were to be a time of testing. Neither side was sure whether problems could be surmounted sufficiently to allow the effort to move forward at an adequate pace. Indeed, both sides remained uncertain whether the Soviet government could continue to finance the project. Nevertheless, once this time of testing expired, there could be no turning back until the project was completed.

Following the execution of this supplemental agreement, Autostroy paid the Austin Company regularly and in full. Metallostroy appointed a new chief of construction, Mr. Tsarevsky. Investigative reporter Boris Agapov was dispatched to the construction site, and his highly critical article, quoted earlier in this chapter, was published in Moscow. Moscow ordered Autostroy to "liquidate all stoppages" by September 10. Early in September the Communist Party Central Committee in Moscow ordered closer party supervision of plant construction. Thirty-nine additional party, trade-union, and Komsomol officials were assigned to the construction site. The Soviets were determined to put things right.[8]

Wilbert Austin, president of the Austin Company, visited Nizhny Novgorod in August and inspected the progress of construction. When he returned to Cleveland he was greatly encouraged, according to a local newspaper article.[9]

Tells City Club Five-Year Plan Will Succeed and U. S. Should Help.

A prediction that the five-year plan for the industrialization of Soviet Russia will succeed and that the present Communist government will remain the stable ruler of the country was made yesterday by W. J. Austin, president of the Austin Co., . . . at a luncheon forum meeting of the City Club.

The largest crowd that has attended a City Club meeting this year heard Austin's speech and broke into spontaneous applause when he said, in answer to a question: "I do not believe we are being disloyal to the United States in helping Russia to better her own conditions and get ahead."

Austin said that his company had found the Russian Soviet officials honorable in all their dealings, and that the company had been paid according to contract for all the work thus far done. He said he felt certain future payments would be according to the terms of the contracts.

An anti-liquor campaign is being carried on by the government as part of its propaganda, Austin said. Some of his posters depicted workers reeling from too much vodka with such phrases as: "The Enemy—a Mark to Shoot At," "When you Drink Your Family Goes Hungry."

"The Soviet government does not believe vodka is good for workers," he said.

Novel methods have been evolved to improve the efficiency of factory workers, Austin said, exhibiting a large chart used in grading workers on the Austin project. At the top of its columns the chart showed pictures of workers riding lobsters, snails, horses, automobiles, trains, and airplanes. If the worker ranked less than zero in efficiency for a certain day, his name was placed in the column under the picture of the lobster, crawling backward. If he ranked better than 100 per cent., his name appeared under the heading of the airplane.

"The customary greeting of the workers, when they assemble for work in the morning, is: 'Well, what are you riding today?'" Austin said.

Austin called the five-year plan the greatest undertaking of its kind in history.

"Whether it is successful in the degree or within the time contemplated by the Russians is not the important thing," he said. "If they suc-

ВМЕСТО ДЕЛЬНОГО И РЕЗВОГО, ПЕРЕД НАМИ—МУТНО-ЛИКОЕ,
РАССУДИТЕЛЬНОГО, ТРЕЗВОГО, БЕЗОБРАЗНО-ПЬЯНО-ДИКОЕ,
ЦЕХУ, ОБЩЕСТВУ ПОЛЕЗНОГО БУРО-СИНЕ-ЧЕРНОМАЗОЕ,
ПРОЛЕТАРИЯ ЖЕЛЕЗНОГО, ГОРЕ-ЛИХО ОДНОГЛАЗОЕ
ДЕМЬЯН БЕДНЫЙ

СТОЙ

ПОСЛЕДНЕЕ ПРЕДУПРЕЖДЕНИЕ

ceed only partly, it will be one of the world's wonderful achievements. "It is my opinion that the plan will succeed. Possibly not to the extent desired by the Russians in the first five years, but it will go a long way toward it. The Russians themselves expect some difficulty in putting their plants into operation when they are finished, but they will overcome the difficulty."

Two posters that Wilbert Austin brought from Russia. One cries, "Stop! It's the Last Warning!" The other says, "Instead of a strong proletariat—businesslike and lively, thoughtful, sober, and useful to society—we have before us a muddy, dark-blue, scandalous, drunken, one-eyed, filthy calamity." Wilbert Austin, whose Methodist denomination had led the campaign for Prohibition in the United States, was enthusiastic about this Soviet effort. The Austin Company Archives

8

"WORKERS CLAMORING TO GET PAID"

When Allan Austin served as assistant superintendent for the construction of the Worker's City, he was in his third and fourth years with the Austin Company. Because his father, Wilbert, insisted that his two sons work their way up through the levels of company employment, Allan's jobs to this point had all been at construction sites rather than in the company office. His sixteen months in Nizhny Novgorod would provide Allan with his most intensive experience in the direct supervision of laboring men and women.

The photographs that Allan took, as well as the letters that he wrote, give evidence of his interest in the men and women with whom he worked. Many of these photographs focus upon the people with whom he worked, not just upon the tasks they were performing. They capture some of the pride that Russian men and women experienced as they participated in this gigantic effort to build a factory and a city unlike any that they had seen before.

Allan Austin outside the company office in the American Village. *Allan Austin Album*

At that time women did not work on construction projects in the United States, so both Allan and Margretta were fascinated by the women who worked alongside the men. They saw the inclusion of women as a positive development, and they used both still camera and movie film to document the competence of women on the job. However, some older Austin Company personnel had difficulty accepting women as equal participants at the construction site. On July 30, 1930, Harry Miter, project superintendent, wrote an angry letter to Autostroy about the lack of male interpreters.

After three months of continual effort to secure an adequate number of male interpreters who can efficiently translate into Russian the orders of our field engineers, we are compelled to bring the true conditions to your attention.

We now have 6 male interpreters for 15 Austin Engineers. In addition to the male interpreters . . . a portion of the female staff of translators have been assigned for field use. They are unable to stand the hard work, inclement weather, and conditions on the job, and they have not proved satisfactory.[1]

Why female interpreters could not endure such conditions when female laborers did is hard to imagine. The probable truth is that older American engineers felt it their duty to protect the comfort of a female colleague with whom they could converse, and they found this burden irritating. As far as Allan Austin's letters reveal, all the interpreters who assisted him during fifteen months were female. His only complaint was that after he taught them the technical language of construction they were rotated away too quickly.

By September, efforts to correct inefficiencies in Metallostroy's labor organization were having some effect. However, deepening Soviet financial difficulties perpetuated a feeling of uncertainty about the future of the construction effort. In a letter to his father after Wilbert's visit to the construction site, Allan made a veiled reference to this problem.

September 26, 1930

Our general business situation seems rather less settled at present than it did two weeks ago. You have doubtless heard more fully on the subject

The young hod carrier *(above, left)* was perhaps a summer student volunteer. Women and men worked together in a cement-mixing crew *(above, right)*. *Allan Austin Construction Album*

Below: Women workers pause for a photograph. *The Austin Company Archives*

A satisfied bricklayer. *Allan Austin Construction Album*

than I could write, but it is merely indicative of the general uncertainty of any situations in this country.

At the City we have six more buildings to the top, eleven in all, and the worst of the labor shortage is removed. Our daily total is now about 1700 workers. But now we have a total lack of joists and of course that cripples much of the possible activity on the new buildings. Work on flooring, partitions, plastering, plumbing, etc. in the first five buildings is going along at a good rate, with two of them nearing completion except for the sash. We have the frames in, and roof waterproofing has now made a definite start.

October 2, 1930

Dear Mother and Dad—

Just now we are being amused by the vagaries of Russian Time. Yesterday according to official notice, Daylight Savings Time came to an end and we turned our watches back to where they had been in the spring. Today comes word from Moscow that this is a mistake and the time should have been left as it was. So we are slightly confused, and for the second morning we have been arriving at the office in sections. Some, of course, forgot the first change and came early; today no one was quite sure about it. It will probably take a Soviet committee some time to decide what time is the right time to change the time, and what time it should be changed to, etc. Meanwhile, any time is the right time.

Today had a distinctly wintry atmosphere, and there are snow flurries, though not enough to stay on the ground. Some of the houses have had heat; our apartment and the Club have none so far. However, we had running hot water last night, and that was encouraging. Our windows are puttied up, the stove cleaned out, and most things arranged for a nice, snug winter.

The monthly progress report on the Worker's City will show a better percentage of work done than any previous month, I believe. This is due to interior finishing rather than any increased tempo on outside work. We remain completely out of joists. That is slowing up eight or nine buildings. We are about to start excavation for the Club on the South side.

October 13, 1930

Dearest Mother and Dad—

I can now allay some fears about the heating system, for in general it is working all right and is equal to any weather we have had so far—which really isn't very cold. On our side of the Apartment we had no heat for several days, for some unknown reason, but this morning it is on again—for good, we hope. We have also had hot water, now and then. . . .

The day before yesterday we received four packages of very fine dried fruits which Mrs. Stroup sent from California for Margretta's birthday. The job is more or less unchanged: the usual full quota of promises and hopes, and radical changes in personnel, but little beyond that. As I see these things repeated so often, I feel more pessimistic now than at any time so far. We are roofing the next five apartments, are out of joists, low on gravel and cement, yet started excavation on the next 30 buildings. What we need most is some, just a little, evidence of accomplishment for our efforts.

Allan

October 20, 1930

Dear Dad—

Today marks the beginning of the second six months that we are in Nijni. As a fitting climax a wonderful thing happened—the linoleum came. More correctly, it has been here in a warehouse for an unknown length of time, but no one suspected its presence until Bill Wolfe happened to find it. Shared among the group it will probably cover most, if not all, of our floors.

Remarkable problems were created by the single-minded Soviet effort to sell goods abroad in exchange for the hard currency needed to finance this construction and other industrial projects.

Perhaps you remember the little sawmill near here on the road to Kanivino. Miter and Wolfe visited it today to see what possibility there is to get joists from it. We have run out at the Worker's City and, to

On the Autostroy job some logs were sawed into joists by hand. *The Austin Company Archives*

complete even *twenty* buildings, we need over 11,000 joists. They found the mill to be turning out the very thing, 5 by 25 cm. boards—for shipment to America! So of course we can't get them.

Incidentally, we are changing our plans and will use 6,000 doors of a different size than contemplated. These were a shipment from England, originally rejected. The Soviets' international trade situation certainly affects a lot of things.

We go on with many petty annoyances that wear one out. The heat is off more than on, simply because teams are not provided to bring wood or peat. Our new crushed brick highway in the settlement is being rolled by a roller that is broken down in the daytime and runs all night. All roads to the City are practically impassable—mud up over the running boards—so we get exercise pushing cars. None of these things is important, but the endless string gets to one. . . .

That same day Harry Miter, project superintendent, drafted a long letter to Austin Company employees at home to give them some flavor of life and work in Nizhny Novgorod. He expanded upon the problem of mud.[2]

I've heard the phrase "Sea of Mud" but I could describe it more aptly as "Sea of Glue." We drove the Buick [Miter's large personal car] up one of the plant roads and trusted the mud too much, finally getting to a point where some hard pushing was necessary to move further. I optimistically helped push from the rear end. The first spin of the wheel forward splashed an even coating from my hat to my feet. I tried to shout to the chauffeur but my mouth filled with mud. He then reversed and repeated the process. Before I could get out of range I had a good many pounds of goo splattered all over my anatomy. . . .

We are all trying to figure out what sort of weather we will have this winter. We hardly know what to expect. Someone told us to stand the steel on end so we could see it through the snow! We are, indeed, planning to erect steel all winter. . . .

In spite of difficulties and daily problems we haven't lost our sense of humor—yet. Our organization has the typical Austin spirit. Difficulties may stop us temporarily, but we never quit trying.

October 26, 1930

Dearest Mother and Dad—

Our weather remains good for this time of year, cool and dry. Each morning it becomes darker and doesn't really get light now until about 7:45. We watch the dawn from the breakfast table. Interesting, but it is sure hard to get up in the dark. . . .

Our heating system is still a bogie-man and worries us all, for with its present intermittent habits it will surely freeze solid as soon as the weather turns cold. In addition, they plan to heat too many barracks from it.

Allan

Apparently the Americans of the village depended upon a central heating system provided by their Russian hosts, and over which Austin Company personnel had no control. The large power plant under construction was designed to supply steam heat and electricity to the Worker's City and to the factory in another year. Meanwhile the Soviets had erected a small central heating station, fired by peat or wood. They intended this to supply heat to the American Village and also to some workers' barracks. The barracks that Allan photographed were long tents, partially dug into the earth or partially

Through the first winter Russian workers made do with temporary housing in excavated dugouts, tents, even caves on the riverbank. *Allan Austin Construction Album*

sheltered from the wind by rubble stone. They had a stove near the center of the tent, but I would guess that on a cold winter night the primary heat came from many bodies sleeping close together. Whatever heat the Americans had, or lacked, the Russian workers surely had less.

In November a reporter for the *New York Evening Post* sent a dispatch from the construction site.[3] "H. F. Miter, construction chief, drove us around the plant. Over the door of the construction office hung a broad sign in mutilated English, 'Workers All World Unite.' . . . That was for the benefit of a little group of American workmen who drifted into Nijny, job hunting. Many of them were Communists." The same article reported that due to an acute labor shortage on the job, the working day had been extended from eight to ten hours. However, from Allan Austin's point of view, there was a surplus of labor, because there was not enough material available to keep everyone productive.

November 1, 1930

Dear Dad—

The weather has been better than we anticipated. The labor power

Two American laborers with their Russian comrades. *GAZ Museum of History*

has increased from about 1,650 to 2,000 at present. This is the largest number we have had on the [Worker's City] job and is more than ample for the materials available.

Outwardly, the Worker's City looks good enough and the progress is about what I had expected, but of course not up to the program which Autostroy requires.

Brickwork to the top on 19 buildings
Concrete Frame finished on 13 buildings only
Roof Construction finished on 10 buildings
Roof Waterproofed on 8 buildings

The first building still lacks about 40% of its sash and all exterior doors, to be enclosed. Plumbers and electricians still have a lot to do. Autostroy is quite anxious to move into this building [from their downtown office] and had set November 1 as the date, but it will be at least a month late. No other building is at all enclosed or in shape for occupancy.

Worker's City construction in late 1930, before winter snow set in. These first five communal buildings, each designed to accommodate 200 workers, were linked by elevated walkways. A temporary railway to move construction materials can be seen in the foreground. The low brick wall under construction is for the "Club House," communal dining, and meeting facilities. All these buildings remain in service today. *GAZ Museum of History*

Over in Unit #2 [the second group of thirty buildings] things have been happening. Considerable amounts of water and sewer lines have been laid, using the trenching machine for this work and speeding it up 500%. All 30 buildings have been laid out, about 10 are excavated, and foundations complete in four. This work is going quickly and we will probably have 20 or 30 foundations ready to work on next spring.

Bread Factory foundations are started, and this building will be built by the Finnish workmen.

Due to the fact that none of the buildings are enclosed, we will be stopped rather completely as soon as real cold weather comes. We are not counting on much progress during the winter, contrary to Metallostroy's opinion.

Allan

Allan was skeptical of plans to continue construction at the Worker's City through the coldest winter months. In this instance Metallostroy would prove him wrong. Meanwhile, work on the Forge Shop, which would be used to fabricate equipment for other units, must somehow be accelerated. Allan feared that money would be wasted there while the workers themselves were not being paid. He was troubled by the workers' plight.

November 5, 1930

I wish we had a simple criterion by which to judge the efforts we put forth on this job. Here every principle of economics and workmanship seems upset, and the results are most confusing. Today, for example, we learned that some work—any kind of work—must go ahead on the Forge

Shop because VATO [the All-Union Automobile and Tractor Association] has ordered 1,250,000 Rubles to be spent on this building before the first of the year. That's intelligent spending for you!

I can hardly write for the din made out in the hall by workers clamoring to get paid. Poor devils, my heart goes out to them, and conditions are worse than I can describe here. . . .

November 24, 1930

We have noted numerous remarks by the Russians that they were pretty cold at times when we were not uncomfortable at all. I think the food has a lot to do with it. A hungry person gets cold a lot quicker. They seem to have plenty of clothes on, most of them, but still they complain about *"zima"* [winter].

Allan heard a new excuse for the Soviets' failure to pay workers at the construction site. "Most people on this job, including officials, are not being paid at all, for over two months. Some confusion about the change of fiscal year from October to January, with no intermediate appropriations. Well, it's all in the life of a good Communist." A subsequent letter, however, showed that this could not be the explanation.

December 2, 1930

It is rather amazing the expense to which they are going in their winter projection and heating methods. As you may know, this "Special Quarter" from October 1 to January 1 is designated to speed up production

The workers' dining room, November 1930. *The Austin Company Archives*

faster than the normal rate of increase for the Five Year Plan. This is achieved by appropriating increased sums to cover ordinary expenditures. By dispersing these sums they feel they are meeting the requirements. Consequently, nothing is too expensive to attempt. On the other hand, the workers are still unpaid. A quarter million rubles is due them at the Worker's City alone. And it is a workers' government!

9

"EVERY PRINCIPLE
SEEMS UPSET"

November 5, 1930

Dear Dad and Mother—

. . . I have nearly finished an article on the Socialistic City, describing the conditions of life anticipated. I would like you to read it and pass on it. My idea has been a non-technical article that would interest as many people as possible, interpreting Russian ideas through their expression in construction. There is a wealth of material here and writing is largely a matter of choice of subject. I would like to take advantage of this material and get in a few literary licks for myself. I also want to be consistent with our business position and ask you to read the article with this in mind. I hope to have some good photos to go with it.

Communism baffled most Americans and frightened many. Allan's essay—much of which we read in the chapter on Worker's City design—conveyed

Soviet aspirations through the design of buildings and the routines of every-day life that they would accommodate. The American reader could visualize how Russians might experience communism in their daily activities. This literary effort was the only essay by Allan Austin to be published in a major magazine during his lifetime. With it he seized an opportunity to attempt "literary licks" on a subject of great interest in America. The result was effective because, having worked daily on construction of the Worker's City, Allan could draw forth the ideology and aspirations that the buildings embodied.

Communism held no personal appeal for Allan. He had been raised in affluent surroundings, and he was eager to follow his father and his grandfather in the family construction enterprise. However, Allan shared with his father Wilbert a surprisingly tolerant appreciation of Russians who pursued with great energy their novel vision of humanity and of social organization. Wilbert Austin, in his speech to the Cleveland City Club, had expressed admiration for Russia's resolve "to better her own conditions and get ahead." Like the Soviets, he was convinced that industrialization was the route to human progress. At a time when Western industrial economies were sliding into the Great Depression, Wilbert admired the Soviet determination to advance rapidly. "If they succeed only partly, it will be one of the world's wonderful achievements."

For his part, Allan Austin, because he worked daily with Russian engineers, interpreters, students, workers, and peasants, tried to imagine the impact of industrial development upon these men and women. He had been educated in architecture, engineering, and management, and he shared with his Soviet hosts the conviction that the design of cities and of residences might indeed shape human behavior. Without endorsing a communist vision for humanity, he was excited to participate in an effort to improve the happiness and productivity of men and women by building a new residential environment.

Nevertheless, during the month that he wrote his essay Allan experienced a disturbing contradiction. The same letter that announced the nearly completed article also complained about Soviet misallocation of resources: "Here every principle of economics and workmanship seems upset." He grieved for unpaid workers: "My heart goes out to them, and conditions are worse than I can describe."

It now appeared that the "Austin Method" and Soviet practice stood in fundamental contradiction. The Austin method was rooted in integrity and in trustworthiness—qualities that determined the means this company employed to achieve high-quality construction in record time. When Samuel Austin ordered, "No beer stains on the contract!" he meant that Austin Company representatives were to negotiate clear-headed, rational agreements with clients. They were never to slip something past a business partner. Samuel disseminated many similar aphorisms to remind employees that shortcuts and moral compromises would not be tolerated. Wilbert Austin's developments in construction technology, and his innovative management system, were built upon this foundation. Customers relied upon the Austin Company to apply new techniques with unfailing competency and to maintain the highest levels of quality while building in record time.

The Soviets, in contrast, focused upon the ends desired and were willing to be ruthless about the means they employed to achieve those ends. Confident that they could reinvent both human nature and the structure of human society, Soviet leaders became impatient with any strategy that did not move swiftly toward the desired goal. In their dealings with Western concerns whose help they required, such as the Austin Company, the Soviets could be trustworthy. But within their revolutionary society the swift achievement of goals overrode all other considerations. On the job, Soviets were willing to change their management strategy frequently, sometimes abruptly. This approach confused and angered the Austin Company engineers who had to cope with the consequences. Allan Austin, trained to value consistency, called this "the usual full quota of promises and hopes, and radical changes in personnel, but little beyond that."

When a project faltered or fell behind, as the Autostroy project had, the Soviets employed ever more radical means to force it forward, confident that the achievement of their goals would make all personal sacrifices worthwhile. At this date workers were deprived of their wages in the hope that those funds, expended instead for materials and equipment, might accelerate the pace of construction despite the approach of winter.

The vast majority of Russians with whom Allan Austin dealt on a daily basis were not cynical. Whether Autostroy managers, young interpreters, or peasant laborers, most embraced the vision of a new society. Because Allan also wanted to believe that this vast effort would benefit humanity, as we have seen, he was baffled when the means employed contradicted the professed objective—"and this is a workers' government!" His father and his grandfather had taught him

The first communal building erected in 1930 (above) now houses "veterans," retirees from the GAZ automobile factory. Another building (right) has been renovated with a fifth story added to accommodate two-story luxury apartments.

that only honorable means could achieve worthy ends. Now he was confused. "I wish we had a simple criterion by which to judge the efforts we put forth on this job."

The discovery of my father's letters from Russia led me to visit Nizhny Novgorod myself in 1998 and again in 1999. I learned a great deal. No social movement achieves its goals altogether, but the means that it employs in pursuit of those ends leave their marks. Nearly all of the apartment buildings erected for the Worker's City in 1930 and 1931 remain standing and useful sixty years later. They testify to vision, to persistence, and to workmanship by Russians and Americans together.

In times of great peril every nation must call upon its people to make heroic sacrifices. To defeat Adolf Hitler, many Americans and many more Russians gave their lives—as their children remember with gratitude and with pride.

However, the willingness of Joseph Stalin and other Soviet leaders to employ repressive and illegal means to achieve idealistic goals—and their blindness to the corrosive effects of such means upon the Soviet system—would corrupt and finally destroy the communist effort. The moral vision of a better life for ordinary men and women was lost. Industrial might, desired at first as a means to that end, became an end in itself, one to which human welfare could be sacrificed.

Capitalism is vulnerable to similar corruption, for this economic theory rests upon the notion that unleashing the greed of each individual will—through the magic of free markets—serve the welfare of all. This is unlikely. As Russians experiment with capitalism today, they discover again that the greed of a powerful few, unconstrained by moral principles or by effective political controls, can rob the masses of the resources needed to rebuild their society.

The Austin Company was unusual even in American society. Its owners and managers desired wealth, but more than wealth they valued integrity and respect. They would not offer a bribe, substitute inferior construction materials, or take other moral shortcuts. They understood that their business depended upon giving full value to their customers. The company's ethics emerged from the religious faith of its founders. Within this brotherhood of engineers and architects, respect was earned by doing work competently and professionally. The company motto was, and remains, "Results, Not Excuses."

America was fortunate that capitalism emerged within a democratic society that had a government strong enough to regulate to some degree business conduct, curb many abuses, and tax the rich in order to provide services for the entire community. However, even Americans can forget how dependent they are upon their religious and moral foundations and upon strong democratic institutions. These are the social tissue that prevents capitalist greed from devouring the society within which it lives.

Today, many in America want to release greed from regulation and to build worldwide capitalist empires beyond the reach of any government. If such aspirations prevail, capitalism may soon bloat, oppress its workers, devour its natural environment, and then collapse—as communism did so recently. No society can survive without moral integrity, nor can a society thrive without an effective democracy that allows the many to restrain the power of the few.

"TO STAY HERE OVER CHRISTMAS"

November 9, 1930

Dear Dad—

You need have no further concern about the food the men in the Clubhouse get. With the new Finnish cook Agnes, they are being fed very well. "Best meals we ever ate" has been a frequent comment. The next thing to try is restaurant service for outsiders so that our wives get a rest now and then.

Last night I finished writing my article on "Socialism's Model City" and I am having Mr. Miter read it over.

Allan

Wilbert Austin placed his son's letters in a black leather ring-binder, which also held several letters to Allan's brother and sister.

November 9, 1930

Dear Don and Margaret—

This is the last of our three day holiday for the October Revolutionary celebration. We didn't see much of the Revolutionary celebrations, but there was lots of marching and soldiers, and signs all over the job, and evergreen trimmings. Almost like a Christmas celebration, but not quite. On the second day everyone had the privilege of contributing a day's free work. . . .

Allan

November 24, 1930

Dearest Mother and Dad—

The famous Russian winter has begun to show itself. From an average temperature of about 40 ten days ago, the thermometer has slid down to 8 or 10 [Fahrenheit] for the last two days. We have two or three inches of snow, which sparkles and glistens a lot under the lights at night. The river froze over entirely yesterday, and today we had skating near the shore where the ice had been forming for several days. Sledges are rapidly replacing wagons on the job, and with a little more snow, sleighs will be used instead of droshkys. The most fantastic fur coats and caps have made their appearance. Every fur-bearing animal from reindeer to Scotch Collie seems to be well represented.

The job is slowing up noticeably, with a marked decrease in production. This is easily understood when one walks around the job and sees the groups clustered around every stove and water-heater. Rather extensive preparations are going ahead for winter work—heating material, etc.—but I believe most of it will be a fruitless and expensive venture.

The Austin colony is being depleted by departures, and we shall probably need some reinforcements. It would be nice to get one or two thoroughly agreeable women here; they seem to be rather scarce.

On the other hand, Margretta said today that in general life here was better than she had expected and that she was quite satisfied with it. I feel the same. We get along all right, have no serious wants now, and most of our troubles are always in the future. The business situation in the U.S. should make us appreciate a steady job. . . .

We just came back from the Club House, and the temperature is 4 degrees F. now, the coldest so far. We are going to flood the tennis court tomorrow to have a handy place to skate.

    Allan

Perhaps due to cold weather, the contentment that Allan reported did not last.

[Undated, but bound next]

Dearest Mother—

    . . . Write to Margretta and sympathize with her over my terrible temper these days. She needs it. Much love to you and Dad,

    Allan

On December 1, Harry Miter exploded in an anguished telegram, over the heads of Autostroy, to the All-Union Automobile and Tractor Association (VATO) in Moscow.

WE HAVE NO HEAT IN OUR SETTLEMENT. NO INTEREST IS BEING TAKEN IN FURNISHING US ANY FACILITIES TO WORK WITH. WE HAVE PROMISES CONTINUALLY BUT NO PERSON WE CAN GET IN TOUCH WITH TO GET SOME RESULTS. OUR MEN ARE ONLY PERFORMING ABOUT FIFTY PERCENT EFFICIENCY NOW ON ACCOUNT OF ABSOLUTE LACK OF INTEREST BY AUTOSTROY. AUSTIN COMPANY[1]

Both VATO and Autostroy replied the same day that a person had been dispatched to search for firewood, now very scarce, to fire the boilers for the American Village.[2]

The period during which the Austin-Autostroy contract might be canceled had now expired. On December 5 the board of directors of VATO resolved "to take every measure" to settle disputes between Austin engineers and Autostroy, and "to bind Autostroy to secure the necessary conditions for normal functioning of the Austin personnel as soon as possible."[3]

Christmas was approaching, a holiday as significant for Americans as Easter is for Russians. Family gatherings are the heart of the celebration, so the Americans in distant Nizhny Novgorod found this to be a lonely period.

Back in Cleveland, the Austin Company, along with families and friends of the people working in Russia, dispatched a large shipment of gifts, decorations, and familiar foods with the expectation that they would arrive at the American Village well in advance of December 25. By late November, however, the shipment was stalled at the customs office in Leningrad.

Allan and Margretta had intended to journey to Berlin for Christmas—the first stop on a winter vacation trip through Central and Eastern Europe. However, as winter deepened and morale within the American community declined, the couple decided that they should delay their trip.

November 29, 1930

Dearest Mother and Dad—

We are confronted with a problem that may change our travel plans. There is a feeling that the Christmas party should be a big one, and with the boxes coming we can easily make it so. Recent departures from here will leave a rather small crowd. So we are urged to stay here over Christmas to add what we can to the day. We may delay our departure about ten days and be here with the folks. It is a question of whether 'tis better to be in a Christian country alone, or with friends in a pagan country. In any case we shall miss home and family more than at any other time.

Allan

December 2, 1930

Dear Dad—

In general the job is coming along pretty well, especially when one stands outside and looks at the buildings. Brickwork is completed on 25, and concrete frame on 20. So we are not far off from our goal of 30 buildings. It is the interior where we are most delayed with plaster, trim, and all kinds of finishing. At present the first building is substantially completed and is partially occupied. The next building is practically completed but has no heat. Beyond this, however, nothing will be finished for some time.

    Allan

December 5, 1930

Dearest Mother and Dad—

It is easy to sleep late these dark mornings, and the rest of the day goes quickly. The sun rises about 9:50 and sets about 90 degrees from where it rose. The weather again is mild and pleasant. Yesterday was a Rest Day, so in the afternoon a dozen of us went skating on the river. The ice was solid all across the river, but smooth only in spots. A strong wind would have carried us down to Nijni in no time, but going the other way was hard work. Not having skated in some years, I was none too steady, and I can feel my exercise today. . . .

The morale of the group is pretty good—strengthening, I believe, in many ways. As I said before, though, Mr. Miter is pretty tired and a vacation would help him a whole lot.

Harry Miter supervised the entire project for the Austin Company. This was Allan's second suggestion that Wilbert encourage Miter to take a vacation. However, it appears that Miter would not leave his responsibilities.

December 9, 1930

Dearest Mother—

We will be here over Christmas without doubt now, as Margretta has been appointed a member of the Christmas committee. We shall leave the day after Christmas and be in Berlin for New Year's Eve.

I received a long, interesting letter from Grandpa, full of details of his recent goings and comings. He said that he felt much better, and that you wanted him to accompany you on your trip to Russia next summer. Are you coming surely?

Allan

A Christmas present arrived from Ida and Wilbert—funds to assist Allan and Margretta with their winter vacation.

December 10, 1930

Dear Dad—

Your letter of the 17th came today and contained a mighty fine Christmas gift from you and Mother. You couldn't have chosen a more acceptable gift for us this year, under the prevailing circumstances. It will surely add a whole lot to our enjoyment. Such a trip will be quite educational too, I think, for we plan to get into some out-of-the-way places and leave the more usual points, especially in the Western part of Europe, for other trips which will come. From this angle we feel that we have the best opportunity to see Eastern Europe, and the season suggests Southeastern, so we shall probably go there. . . .

Wilbert Austin, helping a Cleveland fund-raising effort to assist the needy, had written his son to ask for a contribution. Allan apparently undertook charitable giving in Nizhny Novgorod as well.

In regard to the Community Fund subscription which you ask of me, it is quite all right to put me down for $35. I would like to do more in a time like this, but am already disbursing more than that each month and feel that I have about all I can carry. I will be eager to hear of the final results of your campaign, for they should be quite significant. As a team captain, you have a lot of responsibility and added hard work, but it is a real opportunity for service to the community. I would enjoy a part in the drive if I were there.

Strange things continue to happen right along. We are on the point of losing all of our interpreters[,] who have been ordered to move to the

Workers City (where running water, stores, etc., are not yet available) to make room for more Autostroy officials in Nijni. The interpreters refuse to do so and threaten to return to Moscow where their services are in demand. I doubt if it will come to such a crisis, but this serves to keep the pot boiling.

A vacation into an orderly world will be a fine thing.

Allan

Throughout his life Allan loved to join other men in "barbershop quartets." He contributed a fine tenor voice. Christmas preparations at the American Village gave him such an opportunity.

December 22, 1930

Dearest Mother and Dad—

This is probably the last letter I'll write from Russia for a while. Plans for Christmas are going right ahead. We have our tree, I think we have some turkeys, and the "sore-throat quartet" is coming along fine. Our carols are not all they might be, but when it comes to "Love Me and the World is Mine," we are right there on the closest harmony ever devised. I hope the listeners enjoy it as much as the performers.

Last night was the longest night, and the sun came up at about 10 o'clock this morning in a blaze of glory that was remarkable. We are having about 7 hours of daylight.

Mr. Miter returned yesterday morning from Moscow where he had meetings with Autostroy and VATO over water and sewer plans. Food was scarce there and heat was uncertain. He told me that the general business outlook here is pretty lean now, and the Soviets are adopting a policy of rigid economy that almost certainly defers the starting of any new work, and may seriously impair the completion of jobs under way, including our own.

Allan

One of Harry Miter's duties in Moscow had been to plead for the release of the Christmas shipment, which remained stalled in customs. Late in the evening of December 25, the western Christmas, he reported success in a long telegram to Cleveland. Miter's cable and his subsequent letter tell the story of holiday festivities in the American Village.[4]

We had shipped from the States 13 cases full of canned supplies and five cases loaded with Christmas presents. We had several other cases with office supplies and wearing apparel, making a total of 24 cases. Most of these were lying in Leningrad at the Customs office for several months. We tried all possible means to have them moved to Nijni but for various reasons we were unsuccessful. At the last minute we appealed to the highest authorities and, to our surprise, the whole shipment of 24 cases arrived in Nijni on the 24th of December, just in the nick of time.

They had been forwarded from Moscow in a boxcar by themselves and the car was spotted at 1:30 P.M. just ¼ mile from the settlement. We managed to get a truck, and with the voluntary assistance of some of our interpreters and the Autostroy Agent we had all 24 boxes in Davis's apartment in less than an hour. We transferred the five Christmas boxes to the Club House where they were kept for Santa to distribute later in the evening. The boxes had all been opened at Customs in Leningrad and each individual package had been inspected—the wrappings carelessly replaced. We checked all items carefully and found 95% OK.

The delivery at the last moment did more to revive the Christmas spirit and general enthusiasm than can be imagined. Everyone was wildly excited.

Our Christmas tree was a huge success. In addition to the two strings of lights that arrived in the shipment, we had made another string of 24 lights from automobile lamps, colored by hand, and also a battery of large lights to flood the tree from the underside. The ornaments from Cleveland arrived intact, not one broken. Together with the homemade ones and Russian ones purchased here, they dressed the tree to a Queen's taste.

Everyone joined in the decoration of the tree and the club room. There were wreaths in the windows, bunting overhead, greens on the moldings, colored lights and candles softly illuminating all. The entire colony sang carols. Christmas Eve was as near perfect as could be. After Santa [Miter himself] had distributed the gifts that all of you and our families so kindly sent, it was even more perfect.

Harry F. Miter, in a Soviet studio photograph. *GAZ Museum of History*

Our dinner at 6 P.M. tonight was even better than the Thanksgiving one, with a general feeling of wellbeing. Entertainment followed till midnight. Folks went home happier than they thought they could be in Russia, away from their folks at home.

On the 28th we had all our female translators and interpreters, ten in number, at the Club House for a little party, after which we distributed to them gifts from the Austin Company. They were all interested in the Christmas tree. Some of the Russian girls played the piano and sang songs, and then we joined them in Russian games. Everyone talked at once, of course, and it was difficult to learn how the games ought to be played. Ten girls had ten different ideas on the subject. But it was interesting and we thoroughly enjoyed ourselves.

We had arranged to watch the New Year come, together in the Club

House. About 7 o'clock a group of artists from Moscow appeared at the Club House and advised us that they were to entertain us from 8 until 10 o'clock. This very pleasant surprise had been arranged by the local Soviet Committee. The program was typically Russian and the artists—violinist, pianist, mezzo-soprano and others—were very capable. They would credit any stage at home.

We furnished refreshments to the artists at the conclusion of their concert. We offered them transportation in our cars to the Worker's City where they were to give their next performance. They were grateful, yet they left the Club House reluctantly. We then played cards until the time for Happy New Year greetings. Our party didn't break up until about 2 A.M.—everyone was having a good time! [Since this was an Austin Company party, it is unlikely that any alcohol was served.]

The Russian Orthodox use the old calendar that indicates Christmas Day on January 7. Quite a number of the workers were off the job on that day. In the smaller villages the day was truly celebrated. On January 9 several of our ladies gave a party at the Club House for the Russian children in the American settlement. There were about twenty children present from four to ten years old, including our Patterson youngsters. They enjoyed the Christmas tree, American candy and cookies, tea, and then various Russian and American games for children.

The local Soviet Committee has a clubhouse where they give workers, and also our people, skis and skates for daily use. Nearly everyone has tried skiing and found it lots of fun even though we fall more than we stand up. The Finnish colony at our settlement flooded a low spot for a skating rink. We have used it also.

Since the recent heavy snows our folks have been after me to arrange a sleigh ride. After shopping around, our friend Appleton secured three single-horse sleighs to carry the whole colony. The folks were out two hours and came back to the Club House cold and hungry. Everyone enjoyed the ride and voted for more of them.

This was an unusual opportunity for Americans to experience the popular Christmas song from an earlier era, "Jingle Bells"—"Dashing through the snow, in a one-horse open sleigh. . . ."

Meanwhile, Allan and Margretta had begun their vacation. Because, until the end of November, they had anticipated Christmas in Berlin, gifts and greetings awaited them there.

Central Hotel, Berlin
January 1, 1931

Dearest Folks—

It's the New Year now but we feel more as though we had two Christmases. I told you about the first one in Nijni, but the second in Berlin seemed a whole lot more home-like and much closer to you. We were astounded at the number of letters and boxes waiting for us. Several dozen letters (Margretta got 12 from California) and there were about 6 or 7 packages, and large ones, too. Well, you certainly were good to us again this year and your gifts were lovely. . . .

Allan

11

"WORK ON ICE A METER THICK OR MORE"

The winter of 1930–31 challenged the construction effort. Russian administrative reorganization and the need to reengineer many building components compounded the difficulty of sustaining work during bitter cold months.

As its contract with Autostroy specified, the Austin Company designed the various buildings using American measurements and specifications, on the presumption that structural components would be purchased in the United States and shipped up the Volga River to the job site. However, as the worldwide economic depression deepened, and as the Soviets' shortage of foreign exchange grew more acute, Autostroy purchased building components and equipment wherever they could be secured at the least expense. By November 1930, Autostroy had an engineering department in Nizhny Novgorod that reviewed Austin Company designs and made changes and adaptations where they were necessary to accommodate alternative components. At times this arrangement degenerated to confusion, as this letter from Harry Miter attests.[1]

A few factory buildings were enclosed by the onset of winter, but many were not. The Pressed Steel Building, the second largest on the site, was entirely open to the elements when photographed on February 20, 1931. A later photo shows the roof panels being installed after more snow had fallen. *GAZ Museum of History* (top) *and The Austin Company Archives* (bottom)

November 30, 1930

AUTOSTROY
Nijni-Novgorod
Subject: *Removal of Mechanical Layouts.*
Gentlemen,

We wish to call your attention to the fact that the mechanical layouts of the Machine and Assembly Bldg. which we gave you and which you turned over to V.E.O. [an electrical engineering collective], have been commandeered by the War Dept. and have been taken to Moscow. These blueprints, which are the only copies available, were being used to lay out the lighting, power wiring and other mechanical trades. These projects will be seriously delayed unless we have these blueprints back or another set for use at a very early date.

H. A. Miter

Through the winter Russian and American engineers worked together on plumbing, heating, electrical layouts, and machinery layouts for the Machine Maintenance Building, the tool and die forge shop, the woodworking shop, the spring shop, the Pressed Steel Building, the Machine and Assembly Building, the forge shop, and the foundry. In February Miter complained that the Soviets were not providing enough personnel to get the job done.[2]

February 4, 1931

. . . At the present time the [Russian] Bureau has one Heating Engineer and ten draftsmen (eight females); the latter, however, are not qualified either by sufficient training or experience to carry on work of a design nature without almost constant supervision; and we consider them in the category of "tracers" only. For this reason we believe that we need five Technics to act in the capacity of Squad Leaders to make preliminary layouts, which can be turned over to the Tracers in making the final working drawings and details.

. . . You should also assign immediately four Engineers to work in the Projecting Bureau in collaboration with our Engineers Palmer and Worsham, these men to be experienced in the various phases of the work and especially capable of making up Specifications for the materials required.

During cold weather bricks were warmed in a dryer before they were laid, and one of the concrete-mixing plants was equipped to produce heated concrete. *The Austin Company Archives*

…We cannot guarantee to observe any definite schedule for completion of plans, due to the inefficiency and unreliability of your Russian Technical Assistants who are subjected to conditions (beyond their own control) of improper living and transportation facilities.

Miter's job was to keep the pressure on his Russian colleagues. However, when Allan Austin and Margretta returned at the end of January from their winter vacation—they had visited Dresden, Prague, Vienna, Budapest, Constantinople, and Odessa—they saw more construction progress than they had anticipated.

At home in Nijni
January 30, 1931

Dearest Mother and Dad—

Here we are back again, feeling fine and really glad to get home. It looked homelike and nice when we arrived, better than I had expected. The weather has been variable, there is about a foot of snow, and the temperature is now about -15°F. The heating plant functions normally, which is to say indifferently.

On the job there have been noticeable changes. VATO has a new president and he and our old friend Mr. Makarovsky were here when I came yesterday. VATO has been paying more attention to us than ever before, and Mr. Miter says our position here was never better than it is now.

At the City a few days after I left a fire completely gutted one building, leaving nothing but brick walls and concrete beams intact. It was the ninth building in the first row, and was being plastered, and partitions being built at the time, so it was pretty well along. Heating stoves for the plasterers caused it. We have recognized all along that these stoves, and the careless way they are tended, constitute a great fire hazard. Our best [Russian] superintendent is now in jail as a result since it occurred in his district.

Constructively, there is surprising progress which is more noticeable when one has been away. A temporary central heating plant is on the verge of functioning, and the work of plastering and partitions has gone right ahead. The Bread Factory is almost enclosed. No other work, however, is being done in the second Unit [apartment buildings nos. 31 and higher], due to the uncertain budget for next year.

The Soviets were now paying the Austin Company in dependable monthly installments. Therefore the company Board of Directors voted to give their stockholders—all of whom were either senior managers in the company or members of the Austin family—a special cash dividend, despite the bleak outlook for new construction work in a United States gripped by economic depression.

A very pleasant surprise on our return was the notice of The Austin Company's extra dividend on the first of the year. You are all to be complimented on the courageous and generous action taken at this particular time, and I feel that it must result in a beneficial effect throughout the Company.

A good many of our friends, in their Christmas letters, remarked on our enviable position in this country at such a significant time. Apparently the interest in Russia has become a wave.

Allan

This snapshot conveys Allan's skepticism that winter work could proceed with speed or with safety. *Allan Austin Construction Album*

February 4, 1931

Dear Dad—

You will be back from California and Hawaii when you read this.... Yesterday Margretta developed a bad cold and today was in bed until supper time. There is a good deal of this here now. The Russians seem to have frequent ailments which are not surprising considering their food and cold houses.

We are having a brick stove built in our sun room in order to heat it and that end of the living room. The central heat is quite inadequate these days, simply because they fire only one or two boilers at a time, and our apartment has been quite cool recently. The bedroom never does warm up, but we can get along without that if we have full use of the other rooms.

Another practice which I will try to start is that of going to the Club House for occasional meals, especially on rest days. The men, and I guess Mr. Miter, are not especially in favor of this, but otherwise our wives get absolutely no rest from meal preparation from one month to the next. With a good cook there, and plenty of assistants, it seems the thing to do.

Our weather has been cold, staying about 10 below Fahrenheit zero, and today there is a wind which makes it extremely raw....

Allan

When I was a child, my father sometimes took me with him on visits to Austin Company construction sites near Cleveland. We always talked with two people—the construction superintendent and the second in command, who was called an "expediter." The expediter's stories were often fascinating. His job was to anticipate any difficulty that might cause a delay in the work and to resolve the problem before if affected a tight construction schedule. Expediters loved to tell stories of the extraordinary things they had done to secure scarce materials, pacify workers, or bring equipment to the job even when a snowstorm had closed all roads.

On the Nizhny Novgorod construction site the second in command was Chet Appleton. His title was "chief engineer," but he did not remain in an office supervising the work of other engineers. Instead, he was out in the field where some problem had developed, devising a solution. He was the principal "expediter" on this job. While Harry Miter exhibited a combative personality, Chet Appleton was friendly and outgoing. He had the gift of working together with people to resolve problems imaginatively. He was popular among Russians and Americans alike.

The biggest challenge of the winter season was to complete docking and water-intake facilities along the Oka River. Docking facilities had been woefully inadequate during 1930, and now pilings for new facilities had to be driven through the ice pack, and new docks had to be constructed before the spring thaw. The most urgent task—and the most dangerous—was to install water-intake facilities on the river bed to serve the city and the factory. This required the construction of watertight compartments while water levels were low, river flow was slow, and before the ice gave way. In addition, river banks had to be stabilized before the spring flood, or much of this construction might be swept away.

So Appleton, known as "App," spent most of his winter down by the Oka River. There a different Soviet agency, Vodocanalstroy, managed the labor crews. Allan Austin wrote about a visit to this busy area.

February 4, 1931

Dear Dad—

Yesterday for the first time I went down to see the work at the Water Intake on the river. It was an interesting place and full of activity. At present

Allan captured Appleton's unique horse-drawn plane on motion picture film. After men and horses planed the timbers to tongue-and-groove for a tight fit, a pile driver *(opposite)* forced standing timbers down through ice a meter thick and into the river bottom to form a waterproof crib. Workers then sawed the ice into blocks, removed the blocks, and then pumped the crib dry so that water-intake facilities could be constructed. *The Austin Company Archives and Allan Austin Construction Album* (opposite)

the work is all taking place on the ice which is a meter thick or more. About 800 men, practically all visible at one time, are engaged driving piles, making piling, cutting ice. Trucks are running all over the place.

App and Miter are spending lots of time here because it is something which must be completed when the ice goes out in late March or early April. While the job has every appearance of activity, much of it is in circles, with Vodocanalstroy unable to accomplish much. Nevertheless, investigating commissions from [VATO in] Moscow are impressed with the amount of work going on and can see little basis for criticism.

At present about two thirds of the piling has been driven, and the section around the crib is almost ready to be pumped down. Ten pumps are being mounted. The sheet piling is of 8 inch by 8 inch tongue-in-groove, made right on the ice. App has devised a horse-drawn plane to cut the tongues and grooves—two horses and a couple of men doing the work of 25 carpenters. However, much is still being done by hand and there are several hundred carpenters there. Four pile drivers are at work, operated by compressed air.

Concerning my part of the job, we received some news the other day. There will be no more brick buildings built for dwelling purposes during the coming season. The exact type to be built is still undecided, but it will be a variation on the standard buildings you saw going up, which are similar to the apartments near our settlement. Frame construction with stucco exteriors. Autostroy is operating on a three-month budget, with their appropriation beyond the first quarter still uncertain. So they are unable to plan definitely. Consequently the preparation which we had hoped to be making for next summer's work cannot be done at all, and we simply have to continue with what inside work is still unfinished. There is a good deal of this, of course, but we had expected to be able to do much more.

There is a possibility that this change in the type of construction next summer, working from Russian plans, will affect my work. I might be able to get away sooner, or transfer to another part of the job where American drawings are being used.

    Allan

As February passed Harry Miter became increasingly anxious about the slow pace of winter work, particularly the water intake that had to be completed before the ice broke. One reason for slow progress was a complete reorganization in mid-February of the senior Soviet administration for the job; the consequences of this were poorly understood on the job site. In addition, a new concern surfaced. There were virtually no sanitary facilities for the workers, who were therefore required to relieve themselves on open ground. During the winter human excrement remained frozen, but Miter feared for an epidemic of disease following the spring thaw.

Miter addressed a letter about sanitary conditions to the agency that now supervised Autostroy. Two days later he addressed a senior official in Moscow with a litany of concerns.[3]

February 21, 1931

3rd Building Trust
Nijni Novgorod
Subject: *Sanitary Conditions*
Gentlemen:

The condition with reference to sanitation over this whole operation is very poor. No attention seems to be paid to this matter by anyone.

There are large groups of people all over for whom no proper toilet facilities have been provided. Unless radical methods are taken immediately, there will no doubt be considerable sickness here in the spring.

The Worker's City does not have enough outside toilets at the present time, even for one building, and we know that more than one building is being occupied.

These buildings at the Worker's City will have lots more people living in them than the buildings were designed for. This means that our water and sewer systems will carry more load than was anticipated, and it will be absolutely necessary for you to see that sewer lines are not closed [obstructed].

    H. A. Miter

February 23, 1931

Mr. Chuchin, Member of the Board
VATO Construction Sector
Moscow
Subject: *Progress of Work*

There has been very little progress on this work since I wrote you on February 13th. This is due in part to cold weather and in part to reorganization which Mr. Tzarevsky advised me on the 17th had taken place: that the 3rd Building Trust would be in charge of all construction work, and also that Mr. Mosgolov would be here in charge of Autostroy, in place of Mr. Gorin.

I hope this reorganization will be of help to the work here, and we will do our utmost to see that work progresses as we all want it to. The sooner this reorganization is understood by all, the more helpful it will be in keeping the job moving. This applies particularly to the Supply Department, and to having definite control over Vodocanalstroy and Promsantechstroy.

The work which Vodocanalstroy is doing at the water intake is absolutely not satisfactory to us. They are accomplishing nothing, and no one seems to be interested. Shirin has been away from the job for about a week, and the organization which is here seems to be afraid to go to the intake. They stay in the office most of the time.

Vodocanalstroy is just as slow with reference to the temporary sewage disposal plant for Workers' City. This work should have been completed January 1st. The work is still not completed. The sanitary conditions at the Workers' City are very poor at the present time. Just one outside toilet for everybody, adjacent to No. 10 building. We have every reason to believe that we may have a serious epidemic of sickness on account of these conditions. Yet no one in authority here seems to be interested at all in these conditions.

Promsantechstroy at the same time is very late with their work, and they do not have even the first building ready to turn the water on. I cannot understand why these trusts do not have to perform some work in accordance with Autostroy and Austin requests. They should get material, equipment, and men, and be entirely responsible until their work is complete. For example, this morning Vodocanalstroy came to me and requested that I obtain an electrician for them. I am willing to do this, yet I must also remind them that this is their responsibility, not mine.

With reference to engineering work in connection with mechanical trades, very little progress is being made. We must wait for decisions about how these plans are to be prepared. This is going to hinder completion very much, and there will be displeasure when this work is not completed as it should be.

My last word is to emphasize the serious condition at the water intake. Vodocanalstroy maintains they will finish the crib and the gallery before ice goes out. But their progress certainly does not indicate that this will be done. We are no further on the crib now than we were a month ago. It is the same: lack of interest, equipment breaking down, and any other poor excuse for non-performance of work. There are about 500 meters to the gallery. If this work had been started a month ago, it would have required constructing ten meters a day. Now it requires 15 to 20 meters a day.

    H. A. Miter

The day before Harry Miter wrote the preceding letter, Allan Austin had witnessed the intensity of Miter's frustration.

          George Washington's Birthday [February 22]

Dear Mother and Dad

    ... Mr. Miter is in this office now, trying to telephone someone, with the aid of an interpreter. She got the wrong number at first, of course, and Miter asked who she had. "Can we bawl them out for anything while we've got 'em? I hate to waste a telephone call. They're so hard to put through." Unfortunately it was no one whom Miter knew.

    That beautiful disposition of his has undergone a remarkable change. I hope it is not permanent.

    Allan

Miter's frustration grew when early in March he discovered that the Austin Company had been excluded from important planning conferences.[4]

                            March 8, 1931

AUTOSTROY

Nijni Novgorod

Subject: *Vodocanalstroy*

    Yesterday we received minutes of conferences held on March 1st and also on March 3rd, which were attended by Messrs. Dekabrun, Mertz, Makovkin from Autostroy, Shirin and Drozdovkov from Vodocanalstroy. There are a number of references in these notes which specify data to be furnished by Austin Company.

    We think it very strange that we know nothing about these meetings. We have someone in our office every day including rest-days which is conclusive evidence that we were not asked to either of these conferences. This is the same kind of treatment which we have received with reference to all matters in which Vodocanalstroy has been interested in since our arrival in Nijni. We have tried repeatedly to find out whether our plans were to be used or not, and if not, what plans were to be used. At the present time, as far as Austin Company is concerned, there is no single item on this work which is not in question. If it is your desire to let Vodocanalstroy do all the engineering on this work and be responsible for the construction, please advise us to this effect, and we will be governed accordingly.

There is absolutely no excuse for the uncertainty in connection with this work: either you want us to do it or you do not wish us to do it.

We trust that we can receive a very definite statement from you very promptly.

H. A. Miter

Nevertheless, on that same day, Allan Austin reported surprising progress.

March 8, 1931

Dear Mother and Dad—

You will be glad to hear that App has succeeded in pouring the bottom pad of his Water Intake, and I presume is proceeding promptly with the whole thing. That is an achievement concerning which many of us were frankly skeptical, but now he seems on the way to success. App must receive the credit for getting the job done.

The other night, when he was driving home from the river, a train hit App's car broadside, but he jumped and no one was hurt. The train was moving very slowly, fortunately. The car is somewhat bashed in and will never be quite the same.

Presumably this was Appleton's personal Ford sedan, a hard-luck vehicle. The previous summer, on the day the car arrived in Nizhny Novgorod, Austin Company general manager George Bryant had slammed the car door and broken a window.

Allan Austin reported that one of Joseph Stalin's first "purge trials" had sent an engineer to the American Village.

In the big trial held in Moscow last Fall, the principal figure was a Prof. Ramsin. He was sentenced to death and subsequently pardoned to ten years imprisonment. I learned only today that he is occupying a new house directly back of Sprackling's and is employed on this job. He has numerous O.G.P.U. [secret service] among his neighbors and companions, but he is nevertheless practicing his former profession as an engineer.

As surprising as this is, it is strictly in line with Soviet policy of employing prisoners at their former professions in so far as possible. Usually they work at their jobs during the day, and stay in prison at night. Since they have no identification or food cards of any kind, and of course are watched closely, there is little incentive to escape. They have a steady job and assured food supply during the time of their sentence. It is a little exciting to have such a famous personage in our midst.

Today is "Women's Day." These Russians try to claim credit for everything!

Allan, of course, was making a joke. He was probably unaware that International Women's Day had been an important socialist holiday for half a century and that on this day in 1917 women in Petrograd [St. Petersburg] had marched for bread and for human rights—a march that began Russia's first, and democratic, revolution. Margretta would have heard her mother, an organizer for women's rights, sing "Bread and Roses" in honor of this event, but Allan would know nothing of this.

Tomorrow is Rest Day, but Margretta says that she must be sure to get up in time to reach the store early. They are going to have pork, and there will be just enough for three people. Margretta just made a wonderful trade: three cans of sauerkraut for two glasses of chipped beef. That beef is one of the tastiest things we can have now, and reminds us of home more than any other thing. While neither of us was fond of it there, here it goes 100%. Tonight we also had a very good apple pie made from dried apples.

Allan

Allan Austin's opinion—that Chet Appleton was responsible for what proved to be the timely completion of the water intake and other shoreline

projects—was apparently shared by the Russians. Milly Bennett, an American newspaper reporter who spent time at the construction site later that spring, called Appleton "the Russians' idol."[5] She wrote:

C. F. Appleton is one American engineer who has completely won the hearts of the Russians. He is a big, loose-jointed, affable, glad-handing soul, with a million dollars' worth of patience and good nature in his frank, blue eyes.

"To think," the Russians will tell you, with shining eyes, "he is the only American engineer here who doesn't have a university diploma!"

"What a man! He goes out in his high boots and works with the Russians. He shows us how to do the job."

"That Appleton! He has sympathy! He is just like (most priceless of compliments) a Russian."

The American settlement at Nizhni is full of stories of Appleton's exploits.

This year the water mains of the war chemical plant up the Oka River were washed out in the spring floods. The water supply was cut off from the village nearby, as well as the plant. Construction work was washed away. Several men were drowned attempting to build a temporary dam. The chemical plant sent down the river to the Americans for help.

"We want Appleton!" the Russians specified when their emissaries reached the Americans' camp.

When Appleton arrived he found the river banks covered with helpless, hysterical crowds. They were holding a meeting.

"Why the hell doesn't somebody do something?" yelled the American, busting through the crowds.

"The prosecutor says we can't, because there are men down there," and they pointed to the raging torrent of the turbulent, flooded river.

"Do you think they are still alive?" demanded Appleton. "Oh no," they stammered in reply.

"Well, if you want me to fix the break, you'll have to take orders from me," said Appleton.

The first move was to get the prosecutor off the job.

"Now how about some shock brigadiers," asked Appleton. Five hundred shock brigadiers (these are the best workmen, tried and true, who strain every nerve to keep their enviable place in the shock brigades) fell to work. They built the dam; they stemmed the flood that was tearing away the water supply pipes. They repaired the break.

Appleton went back every day for a week and became the town hero.[5]

Later the Austin Company received a $2,000 contract to supervise reconstruction of these damaged facilities.[6] Milly Bennett returned to Appleton's primary responsibility:

They tell, too, how Appleton, at the risk of his life, went down under the ice of the Oka River with M. Tsarevsky, chief of plant construction, and Willie Suikamen, head of the Finnish-American commune, and directed the workers in getting the water system laid, racing against the spring thaw.

Allan Austin titled this snapshot *"Sabotnik* Work" and wrote, "Our interpreters donate a Rest Day to work at the Dock, doing manual labor of a strenuous sort." *Allan Austin Construction Album*

Installation of the water system, which is to supply the plant and city with 15,000,000 gallons a day, had been delayed. The pipes had to be put in while the stream was frozen and in January, three months late, the work was [finally] started.

It raced along at "Bolshevik tempo," thousands of *subotniki* (volunteers working on their rest days) being pressed into service. The frozen Russian landscape flowered overnight with carmine [vivid red] banners: "If we fail in the intake, no water for the new Ford plant!"

Five hundred thousand rubles' worth of machinery lay on the ice, in danger of being pulled away if the thaw came unexpectedly. For weeks the crews, assisted by the Red Army, worked 24-hour shifts, laid pipe against the breakup. They won. The Ford plant will have water.

And that intrepid Appleton! To hear the Russians talk, you'd think he put the intake in, single-handed.

The Russian directors do not blame the Americans for any delay in the Nizhni construction plan. They admit it was partly due to shortage of labor and materials, failure to use available labor and materials 100 per cent. They admit that they are poor organizers on a large scale and that the American engineers have not been utilized to the fullest.

In April the ice gave way, and in May severe floods on the Oka and Volga Rivers were news even in the United States. But at the construction site the water intake, the new docks, and the reinforced river banks held against the pull of the waters.

May 12, 1931

Dearest Mother—

Apparently through some news source you have become alarmed about the floods here, for yesterday a cable came from Dad asking whether we were afloat or ashore. It did have us worried for a while, but the water has stopped at about 74.85 [meters] and is beginning to recede slowly. It would have taken another meter and a half to flood our floors. The dock, roads to it, and a lot of Kanavino and Nijni were well flooded though, and of course lots of villages bordering the Volga. It hasn't gone down enough for us to hear the full extent of the damage, but in parts of Kanavino it was severe.

In a June letter Allan would add one more interesting story about Chet Appleton on the river. He had found the time to build himself a light, veneer-clad speedboat powered by an outboard motor sent from Cleveland. A race was scheduled for the longest evening of the year.

June 22, 1931

Dearest Mother and Dad —

Last night on the river there was a big event—a race between a challenging boat from Nijni, and App's boat. The fame of the latter has gotten abroad, and someone arranged what might be called a regatta, in which several boats from Nijni came up, all bedecked with red banners and slogans, and bringing what seemed to be members of a sporting club. After several false starts, the two boats managed to start off together.

App finished in about two-thirds of the time for his opponent. His boat runs beautifully now and it is quite a thrill to ride in it. Estimates of the speed range from 25 to 40 miles per hour.

12

"AN OPPORTUNITY
GIVEN BY GOD"

Margretta Austin, following her return from Russia, presented more than thirty lectures to church groups in Ohio and in California, describing life in the new Soviet Union. She did this in part to support her family. The economic depression in the United States was so severe that upon their return Allan Austin—the son of the company president—waited half a year for a new job assignment with the Austin Company.

Allan and Margretta attended church regularly throughout their lives. Their parents and their grandparents were deeply religious. Yet Allan's letters from Russia, and Margretta's speeches upon her return, showed more sympathy for Russian communism than for the Russian Orthodox Church. This was because religious practices in America that responded to industrialization differed sharply from those in Russia.

Allan's grandfather, Samuel Austin, had been troubled by news reports about the persecution of Christians in Russia. Indeed there was reason for concern.

Margretta Austin wore this peasant costume when she lectured in America on the Soviet Union. *Margretta Austin Russia Album*

In 1922 Lenin issued a secret order for the extermination of clergy in order to reduce the influence of the Russian Orthodox Church: "The more members of the reactionary bourgeoisie and clergy we manage to shoot the better." Although the text of this order was not revealed until 1990, its consequences—thousands killed and thousands more exiled—were reported throughout the world. Russia's Western trading partners responded with pressure that brought such persecution to a temporary halt after 1925.[1]

Late in the summer of 1930, Allan Austin wrote a reassuring letter to his grandparents, a letter that they in turn allowed the *Cleveland Plain Dealer* to publish.[2]

Heir of Austin Co. Chiefs Says
Those Who Wish to May Attend Church

Attendance upon church services in Russia is possible for those who wish it, Allan Austin writes in a letter from Russia to his grandparents, Mr. and Mrs. Samuel Austin. . . .

"We have attended several church services since we came here," Allan writes to his grandparents, "and services are held regularly in many churches, principally in the rural districts. Our location is decidedly rural. In these places if twenty or more people wish to retain their church services they may do so, keeping the priest and using the church as before. This policy is a modification of previous Soviet decrees and does much to eliminate the bitter complaints which were going the rounds a year ago. . . .

"The more remote from the cities, the more normal and universal is church attendance. In villages [away from] the railroad the services are conducted practically as they were before the revolution, the only restriction being placed upon the income of the church and the priest's salary, which is small.

"In the cities there is little church-going and many buildings are being torn down to make room for commercial structures or more housing. You have probably heard that Russia was oversupplied with churches, and it is certainly true. In the cities there are several in each block, some small and some large, but never in religion's best days would they have been filled. So now many are being removed, some used as warehouses and some of the best preserved as architectural museums.

"The revolution sometimes seems to have an unnecessary severity and radicalness about it, but if one fully realizes how backward and oppressed the Russians were beforehand, one can sense the reason for their present bitterness [against the church].

"The church failed completely to administer to the spiritual needs of the people and the state failed to provide for their economic welfare in the new industrial world. Circumstances swept past both of these institutions, leaving them standing behind, and inadequate for the needs of

143

their people. And now Russia is trying to catch up with the world with sensational speed and is using sensational methods to do so.

"Our church will do well to examine the failure of this Russian church. The lesson is clear: failure to keep up with the changing needs of the people."

Allan's assertion, that the Russian Orthodox Church "failed completely" to meet the spiritual needs of the people, referred to a history that was more complex than he knew. His conclusion that the church must "keep up with the changing needs of the people" reflected the distinctive perspective of the Methodist Christian tradition.

For eight hundred years the Russian Orthodox Church had been a pillar of Russian nationalism in a way difficult for an American to comprehend. The cathedral in Nizhny Novgorod—seized by the Soviets to store building materials for the bridge leading to Autostroy—had been named for Alexander Nevsky, a warrior prince and wise statesman of thirteenth century "Rus." The Russian Orthodox Church honored him as an heroic saint because he repulsed invaders from Sweden, Germany, and Lithuania.

The other pillar of Russian nationalism had been the tsar, who ruled as an autocrat. Lacking democratic traditions, Russia was poorly prepared when industrialization in the late nineteenth century created new opportunities for skilled workers and expanded the middle class. Each of these groups sought a voice in political and economic decisions.

The Methodist Church, to which Allan Austin and Margretta belonged, had emerged in England during the eighteenth century in response to the world's first crisis of industrialization. Poor rural families migrated to mines, mills, and factories in raw industrial communities, where there were few churches and no social services. Several reform-minded priests in the Church of England, led by John Wesley, held outdoor "revival meetings" in industrial communities to inspire and organize these displaced people. Those who responded to their preaching were assembled into disciplined small groups, where they were instructed in Christian ethics appropriate to the industrial environment: literacy, hard work, family responsibility, thrift and saving for the future—but no alcohol, gambling, or other dissipations. When the Church of England failed

to support these efforts, the Methodists separated into their own churches. Their "method" worked: Methodists became the heart of the skilled working class and of the growing middle class in both England and America.

At the dawn of the twentieth century Russia faced a similar crisis in St. Petersburg, then the imperial capital, and in other cities where modern industries were developing. Within the Russian Orthodox Church there were reform-minded priests eager to strengthen parish life and education, to reach out to industrial workers, to decentralize church administration, and to reduce the church's dependency upon state support. Their movement came to a climax in 1905, just as the Russian prime minister proposed a Law of Religious Toleration that would end the persecution of dissident "Old Believers" within the Orthodox tradition, of Jewish communities, and of other religious sects.

However, Tsar Nicholas II rejected this civil reform, and the Orthodox patriarchs rejected all religious reforms. The tsar and patriarchs reaffirmed the reactionary alliance of "autocracy, Orthodoxy, and nationality."[3] The tsar and the church clung to this intransigent position until the Russian revolution erupted in 1917. "Circumstances," as Allan Austin observed, "swept past both of these institutions, leaving them standing behind, and inadequate for the needs of the people."

Before the Russian revolution it was socialist party organizers—not progressive priests—who gathered industrial workers into communities of support and education, who provided institutions for thrift and for self-improvement, and who encouraged peasant migrants seeking factory employment to abandon habits that would not help them in the urban setting. The author of *A Radical Worker* later recalled, "We were of the opinion that no conscious Socialist should ever drink vodka. We even condemned smoking. We propagated morality in the strictest sense of the word."[4]

When Allan Austin and Margretta saw communists campaigning for literacy and against vodka—causes that their own church championed in America—it seemed to them that the sons and daughters of the revolution were compensating for the failures of the Russian church.

While the Russian Orthodox Church had clearly failed to serve industrial communities, its role in rural and peasant communities is more difficult to assess. Peasant spirituality—which Leo Tolstoy and other Russian writers once portrayed with enthusiasm—expressed itself through the village Orthodox church but was not necessarily controlled by that church. Many village priests were subservient to the local gentry, were agents of the local police, or were ignorant, alcoholic, or corrupt, and these were not held in high regard by their peasant congregations. Nevertheless Orlando Figes—a thoughtful historian of the Russian revolution—concludes that during the revolutionary years, when peasant *soviets* (councils) in the villages took possession of lands held by the gentry and by the church, "most of the parish clergy had either gone or been dragged along with the peasant revolution." Some village priests remained with the people from conviction, some from necessity. Lenin considered rural priests a threat to the ideological monopoly that he wished to impose in the name of communism.[5]

Autostroy construction displaced the village of Monastryka, but the American Village where Austin Company engineers resided was within walking distance of another village, Karpovka, graced by a particularly beautiful parish church. During the spring of 1931, Margretta Austin, following a visit to the

The Karpovka Church in wintertime. After their return home, Allan and Margretta used this photo as their Christmas card. *Margretta Austin Russia Album*

Karpovka church, wrote an essay in which she attempted to convey her understanding of the place that the Russian Orthodox Church retained in village life.

The setting sun sent its rays through the colored glass of the windows and touched the bowed heads of people standing within the church. Red, green, blue and yellow, the patches of color shined on the faded head cloths of the women and on the white beards of the men, giving a hint of the benediction within their hearts. The voice of the richly-robed priest rose and fell, and every now and then the people joined him in a chant-like song, entirely a cappella. This was the heart of Russia. Outside the church flowed the Volga River, "Mother of all Russia."

Yet the minor tones of the music were in keeping with the somber atmosphere. I looked for evidence of former grandeur: the painted arch of the ceiling above, the gold elaboration on the altar, the sheen of gold and silver and enamel on the icons around the walls and on the altar screens. These could be seen only dimly in the colors lent by the friendly sun. The ornate chandeliers were dark: no flickering candles or moving gas jets, for the church was now too poor to light these.

How could this handful of people maintain this church? Poor, thin and old, they had all they could do to provide food to keep themselves alive and enough clothes to come to church. For in this land the old have been forced to step aside for the young. The fruit of the land is assigned, not to old and feeble peasants, but to young, sturdy workers who assist their country's salvation.

These workers consider themselves enlightened: free from the fear of punishment after death, convinced that Russian churches exploited the people during the old regime.

So every Sunday evening only a remnant of old peasants gather to worship, feeding their hungry souls with the crumbs of comfort that they receive from the church. Who can tell why they come? I could gather nothing from their faces: the patient, resigned faces of Russian peasants.

Their priest has now descended to the lowest rank in the village. Denied even the small food ration allotted to others, he depends upon whatever his poor parishioners can gather for his living. I wondered what he thought as he patiently read the service. Among the thousands of priests there must have been some who were dedicated to the good of the people, yet history suggests that these were few. Whatever they may have been in the past, one can only feel sorry for them now, struggling against insurmountable obstacles. Although, according to present laws, twenty people who still wish a church may retain it, the government watches closely for signs of exploitation or of gain by the priest.

Year by year, as the aged die of hunger, disease, poverty, and old age, the congregations will dwindle until the end of the old Russian church can be seen. Then what?

I walked out of the church and onto the square. A crowd had gathered there during the church service—hundreds of children with their teachers and leaders. They were listening to a speech. Across their small chests the children carried placards: bold letters announcing their desire to learn and rebuking their elders for illiteracy.

Of course these parents never had the chance to learn when they were young, but there is no effort to portray this to the children in a sympathetic light. To campaign against illiteracy is admirable. Yet the Russian government is using this campaign to break the ties that bind the child to the parent. When children learn scorn for their parents' lack of education, they are more likely to scorn their parents' social, economic, and religious views also. When children are gathered here to protest against their parents, this is part of an organized revolt against parenthood being conducted throughout Russia. The Communist overthrow of the family is not widespread yet, but the government is working toward that end.

If the children were not mobilized in the square, would some of them be inside with their parents? Although it is against the law to take a child into the church, children are permitted to enter of their own accord. I have seen children in the village churches.

Among the young adults whom I have met, none of the bright ones are in church, nor do they believe in it. It is too imbedded in the past. The young people are leaving their families and homes in the villages and are going to the cities where a new Russia is growing. There they learn Communism.

Posters are the most characteristic expression of Russian art at the present time. One shows Easter on the calendar with a man, obviously very drunk, lying in the gutter with a pig. The claim that church holidays are only an excuse to get drunk is one of the most effective arguments. It is true. Around us people still celebrate their church holidays, and for the men this means a vodka spree for several days.

Though I hate some consequences of this removal of religion—lax marriage and divorce laws, and an attitude of contempt toward the sacred—yet I believe that this is a temporary phase in the life of Russia, suited to this generation. It is preferable to the immoral and sacrilegious use of Christianity in the old regime.

Today, young Communists expend a "religious" zeal to build a new country. They worship, not God, but an opportunity given by God to help their country. I see no reason to quarrel with that.

When religion returns in the future it will express the needs of an intelligent and literate people on their way to a better future. The youth of a future generation will have the thrill of revolting, in their turn, against the ideas of their parents—this time a revolt away from atheism that will bring into being a new church.

The Russian people are essentially religious. Their literature shows this introspective, brooding side—deep convictions and deep doubts. Just now the doubts are triumphant, but I feel that the changes of today must lead toward an ultimate good. I credit Russians with supreme courage and unqualified zeal in carrying forward their ideals.

Margretta Austin—young, American, Christian, intellectual—could sympathize with young Russians who abandoned the Christian tradition to pursue their communist dream. Austin Company engineers—most of whom were religious, and all of whom took capitalism for granted—could cooperate with the Soviets in a utopian effort to build a new city for a new Russia.

Yet these same American families had difficulty worshipping with Russian peasant Christians. Here was a cultural gap that seemed too broad to span. In an engaging letter home, Allan Austin told the story of their attempt to join the Easter service in the same Karpovka church that Margretta described. Following the service, as the Americans walked homeward across frozen ground, Chet Appelton led them in a familiar song.

Give me that old time religion,
It's good enough for me!

By "old time religion," Appleton did not mean the ancient rituals of Russian Orthodoxy. He meant the plain Methodist services—just songs, a prayer, and a sermon—that were familiar to these Americans from their childhood.

April 12, 1931, Easter Day in Russia

Dearest Mother and Dad—

After seeing and hearing both religious and anti-religious phases of life in Russia, we can only join with App in singing, "Gimme that Old Time Religion, it's good enough fo' me."

We have been keeping a close watch on the activities of both sides, for Easter is a big thing with both the pros and the antis. So, to see the real Easter service we went down to the little church in Karpovka last night for the midnight service. We started out about 11 and had a nice walk under the starry, frosty sky, and only a few mishaps with thin ice and mud puddles. When we arrived the church was filled with people standing in all parts of it, crowded together so they could scarcely move. Many were holding lighted candles.

We wormed our way up on a tiny balcony at the rear of the church and had a good view. The balcony seemed to be for children and our presence there attracted them in great numbers. We were soon completely surrounded and the objects of much curiosity. They were quite noisy. In fact the whole church was humming with conversation.

We had thought a service would begin at 11:30 and come to a climax at 12, but we waited and waited and nothing at all seemed to happen. The air grew foul and blue from hundreds of people closely packed beneath us. At 12:30, we had just about decided to leave when there was some commotion, and a procession formed bearing banners taken from the walls of the church, a lantern, a cross, and one man carrying a loaf of bread. The procession came down the church and out into the night. Then they circled the church and came again into the vestibule.

There was a long pause, and again we were ready to leave, for my head was splitting from the heat and other Austin folks felt the same. We made our way down the ladder-like stairs and elbowed toward the door. But we were prevented from going farther because the procession was ready to enter the church again. After a good deal of singing in the vestibule, they came in.

By this time we were practically in the line of march and we were pushed back by main force as the procession approached. We were all ready to suffocate or be crushed to death from the pressing and the pushing. Following the procession came a horde of people, some of whom had gone out with them at first, and others who apparently joined the procession outside. They all kept pushing into a church already completely full. The crush was dreadful: impossible to try to get out, with hundreds outside trying to get in, and equally impossible to stay there any longer and be trampled or squeezed to death.

So we attempted to get out. I don't believe I was ever in such a jam, and I hope never to be so again. After about fifteen minutes of most strenuous effort we covered the twenty feet to the door and were again in fresh air.

It was like so many Russian experiences: interesting, different from anything else, but not something to do again very soon. There was little of the mystic pageant, the fine music, and the glamour that had tempted us to go and watch. There was much of the dullness, dirtiness, and delay that one becomes accustomed to here. Most people could see nothing of whatever ritual was being performed at the altar, and none took part in the service, except to cross themselves from time to time.

Yet never in the palmiest days of religion could there have been a service better attended than this, for it was an impossibility to get more people into the building. We would learn that this was the same in churches throughout Nijni.

So we walked home and when we arrived it was nearly two o'clock. In the struggle I lost my only cap.

Russian Easter is by far the most important Church holiday celebrated, indeed the most important holiday of any sort for the people as a whole. It is celebrated for a minimum of three days, and many people take a week following Easter. It is a release from the privations of Lent, for during Lent a religious person has a very restricted diet without meat, milk, and various other things. Afterwards, of course, a lot of vodka is consumed.

Until recently we had not seen a lot of anti-religious demonstrations, but these have made their appearance at this season. Many things were done to divert the people from church-going, although no effort was made to prevent the services themselves.

Galina Moleva stands in front of the beautifully restored Karpovka Church in July 1998. Moleva, the daughter of a Communist mother and a privately Christian father, returned to this church for her baptism shortly after the fall of communism. She would translate this book for Russian publication.

Демонстрация рабочих в честь Партконференции Автостроя.
Автозавод 16/III 3/г. № 716

For example: Our store, which usually closes on Sunday, was required to stay open because no Rest Days are permitted on former church holidays. So people are required to work on both Easter and the day following. The newspapers announced that there was no Easter this year. The radio broadcast a competing program most of the night, and in Kanavino a big sheet was hung outside the station so movies could be shown. No bank withdrawals were permitted for several days before Easter and the sale of vodka was restricted. (There's no bad without some good, you see.)

Please buy me a gray cap. Mail it in a Company envelope, for they arrive unopened.

Allan

Workers rallied outdoors in bitter cold on March 31, 1931, to honor the Communist party. In the foreground are two Ford Model AA trucks from the practice assembly line in downtown Nizhny Novgorod. Behind the workers stand the skeletons of huge new buildings far from completion. *The Austin Company Archives*

13

"HERE THEY WILL FAIL OR TRIUMPH"

As the deep Russian winter continued into March 1931, food supplies dwindled in the American Village, and spirits sagged. Nearly a year earlier, when the Americans first arrived, Margretta Austin had taken the lead in efforts to raise morale in a colony challenged by cold and food shortages. Now she revealed her own discouragement, in a letter preserved by her father-in-law along with Allan's letters—although she tried to put a bright face upon her apologies and her complaints. Another of the American women had broken under the strain, and Margretta wanted her sent home.

March 15, 1931

Dearest Mother [Austin],

I am so glad that you and Daddy had the fine trip to Hawaii. I hope you have the wanderlust for another trip to Russia next summer. We can do better by you this time, as conditions are better—with us, though not with the Russians. I would love the opportunity. I didn't do all that I should have last summer, or all that I wanted to, and can only lay it to my foot not being well, for I know that my spirit was willing. Give me another chance and I will try to make you very happy. I think, too, that Allan and I are much more adjusted now than we were then, and things do not bother us as they used to. Anyway, we are happy, and expect to be for many years to come. . . .

My mind is a bit mixed up today, I find. Allan has been fed-up the last week or so. I think that he is homesick. But he gets over those spells. Everyone here is well just now, though there has been an epidemic of colds and sore throats. Allan has escaped, but I had a bad cold, and then a sore throat that hung on for several weeks. The weather alternates between lovely sunny days and cold, damp, windy days.

We are all dreading the thawing weather with its mud and the variety of smells and filth that will be uncovered by the melting of the snow. It will be terrible. Thank heaven that our immediate vicinity is fairly free. How Allan will be able to stand working at the City is more than I can see.

It may be that, in this colony primarily of men separated from their families, stories of sexual indiscretion and alcohol consumption were beginning to circulate—things that this upright group could not deal with smoothly. Margretta blamed one woman for fanning this gossip.

Our biggest difficulty now is personalities. On the whole the women are getting on much better than ever before, and there is little gossip among them, with one exception. The men, on the contrary, are indulging in the worst kind of gossip, and that is unfortunate. Yet Mrs. P[atterson] is really going beyond the bounds that anyone can stand. Knowing that she is neurotic we felt rather sorry for her, but she is stirring up so much trouble, and trying to do more, that she really is a menace. She is consorting with the worst gossips among the men, and they pass around the worst bunch of lies. It will be terrible if these things get back to the families of the men here. Today L [Kempler] and I have had to tell our maids that we are not at home to her. We had heard some things she has been saying about the four of us—the Kemplers and Allan and I—things that only a diseased mind would imagine.

The Colemans have refused to play bridge with the P's, so our bridge club is gone. Mrs. P broke up our afternoon current-events reading club, and so on. Mr. P is very unpopular with the men, and no one can work with him. They undoubtedly should not be over here.

Last night there was a concert at the Russian clubhouse—a violinist, and a singer, both women. The former was good but the singer was terrible. We enjoyed it although we had to wait for an hour, while they tuned the piano, before it began.

Then we went to the [American] clubhouse. Smitty [E. T. Smith] delved into his Christmas food and we had a grand spread: canned chicken, deviled ham, sardines, cookies, and tea and coffee. We sat around and talked until after midnight. Bill Wolfe said that we would remember these times for a long while.

There has been lots of skiing lately; it takes up all the rest days. One day I fell going down hill and hurt my arm, and it has been sore for a couple of weeks. It is almost well, but I am afraid I can't ski any more. Allan went out some, but not often. . . .

Dearest love to all of you,
    Margretta
P.S. Allan approved what I wrote about Mrs. P.

Two days later Allan was in a good mood when he wrote to his sister, Margaret. She had sent him a birthday greeting that reached Allan well before April 1. A few days later Allan wrote a letter to both Margaret and his brother Donald. Margaret was in her first year at Connecticut College for Women, while Don was in his final year at Yale University, not far distant.

                                                        March 17, 1931
Dearest Margaret—
    You were first under the wire with birthday greetings this year. Thank you for your good wishes and love. Today is our twentieth-month wedding anniversary, which makes us feel old and experienced. Margretta

retains her youthful beauty just the same, and is quite spry and in full possession of her faculties.

Don's report shows that college is doing for you what it should: it is supposed to be a transition from adolescence to adult. While it is nice to be sixteen and unkissed, it is nicer to be twenty-six and married to Margretta. Just go on growing up and when we get home we'll like you more than ever.

I have a new interpreter, a girl 20 years old, just out of the Foreign Language School in Moscow. It is a tough job for her, and keeps me busy explaining words. Just imagine yourself with a fairly good reading knowledge of French, for example, suddenly taking on a job as interpreter for some French engineer who talks in terms which you do not know even in English. Marusa is in the same fix. She learns quickly. But she is only going to stay six months and then return to Moscow, so about the time she becomes useful, she will leave. Well, perhaps I shall also leave about that time.

We have been having a little trouble with solicitous Tom cats. The Wolfe's had a young lady cat which was the object of their attentions, and they would park out on the back porch and woo her most heart-rendingly. Last night before going to bed I took a bat and went out to woo them myself. In administering some treatment, I made a wild swing and wrenched my back. Today I feel every movement, and think of the cats. But last night we slept for a change.

Allan

March 23, 1931

Dear Margaret and Don—

Our Spring has come for certain today, with the snow running away in streams, and the promise of mud underneath. In a few days the bridge to Nijni will be taken up, and probably within ten days the ice on the river will break up. Summer is still a long way off.

Don, it was good news to hear that you are going to Harvard Business School next year, if they are willing.

Tonight we are having a community dinner at the Club, guests of

Mr. Miter. And in a few days he is leaving for Berlin to meet Mr. Bryant there. They will probably not be back here until the middle of April. Mr. Miter has had a bad case of sore throat and laryngitis. He needs a vacation very badly.

You should see the big blocks of ice they have cut from the river and hauled up to our new ice house. The river froze to four feet thick, and these blocks are cubes about that size. They must weight over a ton.

Allan

March 29, 1931

Dearest Mother and Dad—

You will note that we left New York just a year ago today. Right now it seems longer than that, for things are very dull here. Rest Days, of which today is one, are getting to be more monotonous than work days, for there isn't a thing to do that we haven't done many times before. That is the principal difficulty. We have plenty of reading, etc., but have been reading so much that there is little diversion in it any more. The same with our bridge and other parties: the folks are just the same and do the same things and talk about the same topics. Well, we aren't going to die from boredom. But time passes slowly right now.

I am enclosing an ad for a book that sounds good. I am convinced that a background of Russian history is necessary for a clear understanding of what we are seeing here. I have read two or three already, and this one sounds worthwhile.

For my approaching birthday Margretta is having as swell a dinner party as possible. Yet two birthdays away from home seems like a long time. My gray hairs have increased 100%: I now have about 6.

Last night we played bridge and I managed to win a prize—a little mouse trap, very useful and acceptable. A real imported U.S. one, too. I have been watching the pages of the *Saturday Evening Post* for my article, but in vain so far.

Allan apparently had some expectation that the article he had written in November, "Communism Builds Its City of Utopia," might be published in the *Saturday Evening Post*. This was America's most popular magazine, and also one in which the Austin Company advertised. Instead, the article was published in August in the prestigious *New York Times Magazine*.

An interesting local item is that the schools have closed for a week because the mud makes it impossible for the kids to get back and forth.

And an event of major importance was the securing of a full dozen fresh eggs from the Old Lady in Monastyrka yesterday. That alone will add much to the success of the forthcoming dinner party.

I have positive proof of the Tartars' fondness for horsemeat. This morning when I went down to the river to photograph the new barges before high water came, I chanced across a few hoofs and what-not near the huts in which they live. Not that there is anything wrong with horsemeat—except toughness—but this shows we are living among exotic peoples whose ways are not our ways. The Tartars have achieved efficiency in the art of living, since they are teamsters by day.

I almost forgot to tell you that we have just gotten Venetian blinds for our windows, which will help a lot in the long days. They were here in a warehouse, no one knows how long . . .

Best love to all of you. We are feeling fine, except when we think too much of our troubles.

Allan

April 12, 1931

. . . A new development may revolutionize our lives here. The store has received about eighty crates of real oranges, and we each had an orange for breakfast. They were simply delicious. The price hasn't been established yet but we are eating a few before we find out that we can't afford them. We also hear rumors of lemons, tomatoes and other fresh vegetables en route from Moscow especially for us. This year Moscow has received shipments of fresh vegetables from the south, earlier and larger than last year. We are all thankful.

Otherwise our food supplies are pretty thin. About half the folks have nothing left, and it will be six weeks at best before the next U.S. shipment arrives. Recently the store hasn't had a single vegetable available, not even cabbages. So a few oranges and tomatoes will do us all a lot of good.

We had not heard a word from Mr. Miter until this morning when a telegram came, five days old from Berlin, saying he and Bryant were arriving in Moscow on the 10th and will be here tomorrow.

May 12, 1931

Dearest Mother—

The work at the City is speeding up somewhat and we now have about 2500 workers. Also about the same number are living in the buildings which are (more or less) completed. So we have furnished some housing anyway, and will soon have a good deal more ready.

They are planning rather large amounts of housing construction for this year, but most of it is of a modified type, or simply frame buildings like we live in. I really don't think that there will be a lot that we are responsible for.

So if you come over next August, we may go home with you. I, at least, would like that arrangement.

Much love to both you and Dad,

Allan

As people moved into fifteen not-quite-completed buildings in the first row of the Workers' City, profound changes were taking place in the design of the third row, the fourth row, and the remainder of the city. To place these changes in context, we can consider the second half of Allan Austin's article, "Communism Builds Its City of Utopia," which he had drafted the previous November. The first half was quoted in chapter 5. Allan wrote as though the projected streets and public buildings were already in place.

The city as a whole covers an area of about 3.66 square miles, has an extreme length of three miles and contains about twenty-five miles of roadways. It is so oriented that each building has an east and west exposure, getting direct sunlight into every room. A large central square forms the hub of the city. Here is the Palace of Culture, which supplements the

Shiny helmets were worn by firemen who rode the truck, while those who followed with horse-drawn equipment wore caps. *The Austin Company Archives*

functions of the clubs and is the administrative headquarters for all cultural development throughout the community. Adjoining this building is the governmental and political headquarters and on the other side of the square are situated a department store and a hotel. The fire department occupies a prominent corner, as is fitting for an organization whose members are on a par, roughly speaking, with the Governors of American States. The brightness of their brass helmets establishes their position in no uncertain way.

From the central square a double boulevard about a mile and a half long runs to the Oka River, where there will be a yacht basin and docking facilities for the river boats. The boulevard runs through a park, which comprises about one-third of the entire area of the city and which has sites for a university and future public buildings. At one side of the city and convenient to the industrial plant are various service buildings, including the kitchen factory, the bread factory, the slaughter house, the laundry and bath house, and food-storage buildings. Well isolated from the city proper and in attractive wooded surroundings is a polyclinic hospital. A large athletic field has one stadium big enough for football and track events, a smaller stadium for tennis matches, and locker and bath houses.

The hours of work and leisure in the Russian Utopia will probably be much the same as those of working people in the United States. The eight-hour day is in effect rather generally, with a seven-hour day being introduced in some places. Some figures I recently saw indicate that out of about 16,000,000 organized workers in the Soviet Union all except a little more than 1,000,000 were working eight hours a day. This is the length of the work day in the city under construction. One hour is generally taken for lunch. Lunch rooms in the industrial plant, supplied from the central kitchen factory now being erected near the city, will serve the noon meal, making it unnecessary for the workers to carry a lunch or return home for it.

Recreation after working hours will probably consist largely of sports, for there is a great popular interest in games, gymnastic drills and all sorts of out-of-door activity. The entire field of sports is enthusiastically encouraged by the Soviets and is characteristically fostered by the formation of outing and sporting clubs, to some of which are assigned instructors. I was surprised to observe the complete stocks which sporting goods stores carry, in contrast with the meager variety of wares in the average store. And it is interesting to note that most all sport terms are English words. Tennis and volley-ball are popular. The proximity of the river makes swimming and boating in Summer very convenient, and with but few exceptions the condition which Will Rogers summed up as "not a bathing suit in Russia" still prevails. There is an organization called Dynamo which fosters all kinds of sports, organizes teams and competitions and occasionally sponsors a tour of foreign athletes through Russia. Recently we witnessed an exhibition of boxing by a group of Swedish boys, followed by an exhibition of "physical-culture" put on by the Dynamo group.

The Russians, workers and peasants alike, seem to have a passion for singing—beautiful minor harmonies which are wholly unlike our music. This singing, with accordion accompaniment, is to my mind one of the most attractive features of Russian life. Every night, now that it is warm weather, we hear groups of men wandering about singing. There used to be a great rivalry between the villagers over their singing, and each village would have its characteristic song. Since much of our labor comes from these villages, we still hear the old refrains.

If family life among the workers now engaged on the model city is an indication of what may be expected later on, I should say that it would be, from our point of view, quite normal among the older engineers and mechanics. There is, however, a large group of young people of both sexes—apprentices or "Komsomols," who have left their parents' homes and are embarking on careers of their own under the guidance of the Soviets. Their presence in large numbers is probably the most noticeable feature of the social life, and they are most typical of what might be called the New Russian. Stepping into one of their rooms, one finds the walls covered with revolutionary posters and pictures of Soviet leaders, and on the tables are pamphlets of the same order. As I said before, there does not seem to be any system of chaperonage, and the young people's morals are their own concern.

As a footnote to my mention of family life, I should add that in spite of the publicity usually given to the subject of birth control by journalists writing of Russia, there is not the slightest evidence of race suicide. There are babies in abundance and the nurseries and kindergartens should have plenty of customers.

To sum up: sports, amusements, home life, education, work, all phases of existence in fact, are here molded to fit the socialistic concept. This doctrine will soon be practiced here on a scale never before attempted, with people educated to it for a decade and under conditions as favorable as can be prepared.

Sitting here in the midst of construction activities, one is apt to become absorbed by the problems of providing housing and complete facilities for 30,000 persons in a year and a half, of the shortage of skilled labor due to the unprecedented amount of construction now under way in the U.S.S.R., of the corresponding shortage of materials, and dozens of other distractions quite familiar to any one working in Russia. Perhaps the carpenters never worked on any but log houses in their own village before; perhaps the plasterers were laborers at the dock three weeks ago, before they went to school a few nights; perhaps an electric saw is new to every one. Well, so is a socialistic city new to them all, and if they are to obtain the unusual benefits and vastly improved living conditions which have often been promised them, they must resort to unusual methods and make unusual sacrifices to achieve these extraordinary ends.

Is the game worth the candle? Will the experiment succeed? No prudent person is answering these questions at the present time. But the socialistic city at Nizhni Novgorod is giving to the Soviet Government a proving ground for its theories. Here they will fail or triumph. They have not had this chance before.

By comparison with the utopian vision expressed in the design by the Moscow High Technical College and "rationalized" by the Austin Company, the Workers' City was changing. At least one of the first buildings completed was used not for housing but for Autostroy offices. Because of an acute shortage of worker housing, workers and families were crammed into buildings as they became available—indeed, before they were completed. On February 21, Harry Miter reminded the Third Building Trust, now overseeing Autostroy, that "these buildings at the Workers' City will have lots more people living in them than the buildings were designed for" and that this would require keeping all sanitary systems in first-class condition.

For the vast majority of workers unable to squeeze into the new apartment buildings, housing was primitive—in many cases, appalling. Peasants, recruited from villages where work was scarce and hunger prevalent, had little choice but to endure these conditions. However, the skilled workers vital to the swift completion of construction were difficult to retain, for there was keen competition for their services among the many ambitious projects of the first Five Year Plan. As winter intensified during the opening days of 1931, reporter Boris Agapov wrote that half of the skilled workers thus far acquired had "disappeared from the field of view" or "dispersed to other enterprises." Autostroy was scheduled to receive fifty additional specialists that month but had "absolutely no idea where to put them." Even the plans drawn to date would accommodate only two-thirds of the workforce projected for the automobile plant once it was in operation. By summer, when the construction labor force swelled to its peak, living conditions for some were in such "catastrophic condition," according to another newspaper report, that workers "ran from the construction site."[1]

Therefore it is not surprising that some workers—as reporter Milly Bennett observed in June—occupied not-quite-finished apartments by stealth or by force.

166

The Russian workers come to the plant from the villages, husky peasant men and women, with packs on their backs. They live in long, rude barracks. And, impatiently, they move into the unfinished model houses of the Workers City, 300 families strong, and camp there.

What though the builders tear their hair and cry: "But the electric fixtures aren't in yet! The plaster is still wet on the walls!"

For if the worker has moved in his bundle and bed, put a lock on the door and his primus [stove] in the kitchen, all the American engineers on earth can't budge him—nor break the Soviet law which says that a worker on a job cannot be moved from one room until you give him another just as good. So the workers stay and the 200 apartments remain unfinished.

Bennett reported further that in the communal buildings "there are workers' cots in rows in the halls, people camped in the laundries, each with a primus."[2] According to the recollections of "veteran" workers who occupied these buildings while they were new, there was immediate dissatisfaction with these communal buildings. The toilets, showers, tiny kitchens provided at the ends of the hallways were inadequate. Both individuals and some families that found themselves in these buildings resisted dependence upon the collective facilities for bathing and dining provided in the adjacent communal buildings. Yet attempts to cook and to eat with roommates made the small rooms seem tiny indeed.

My mother told me of difficulties persuading peasants in the family buildings to use the bathtubs provided for washing rather than for coal storage. Mother attributed this to ignorance on the part of people who had never seen such facilities, but it may also have been prudence—they did not trust the central heating system supplied by the power plant. It may be that Boris Agapov's vision of "a city without chimneys and stoves, . . . sky not spoiled by soot or smoke," was not fulfilled.[3]

The flat roofs with internal drainage—a common industrial design in America—were not well maintained, and they soon leaked. Nevertheless, the accommodations in these buildings were not only the best available, they were the finest that many workers had ever seen. In July 1998 the author met Nickolai Makhov, a retired autoworker who began a long career by helping to complete some of these original buildings after Allan Austin departed. Then he lived in the buildings for many years. "Some of us," he told me, "had lived in holes in the ground. We loved these buildings. We used to dance on the roof!"

It was the communal living units, the first five buildings in each row of apartments, that embodied the utopian vision for the new Soviet man and woman. These five buildings—joined by passageways and linked to common dining and recreation facilities, nurseries, and kindergartens—were designed to relieve men and women workers from domestic responsibilities such as cooking and child care, and to ensure that the next generation was raised primarily in communal rather than family settings. Allan Austin's description of the Soviet's utopian vision, quoted in chapter 5, related to these buildings in particular.

Four rows, each composed of fifteen apartment buildings, were eventually constructed, and each row began with five of these communal buildings and then continued with ten apartment buildings for conventional families. In fact, however, only the first set of five communal buildings, begun in 1930, were equipped with covered passageways between the buildings and the full complement of communal facilities for dining, recreation, and child care. When construction resumed in the spring of 1931, plans for such communal-support facilities for rows two, three, and four were cancelled. This was probably an economy move, considered temporary at the time, but in fact the planned communal facilities were never built. Without them, the communal apartment units remained cramped and uncomfortable, with inadequate sanitary facilities.

The family buildings behind these had been designed to be crowded: they constituted two-thirds of the initial housing units, but they did not express any fresh Soviet vision. Three families shared four-room units: one room for each family plus a shared bath and a common room for eating.

When housing construction resumed in the spring of 1931, Soviet engineers gradually redesigned the buildings in rows three and four to reduce costs, speed construction, and ensure that Russian labor could complete the work after American engineers departed. More wood frame and stucco were used, and less brick. The architecturally distinctive Austin-designed stairwells disappeared from the family buildings. On the fourth row, completed after Austin engineers departed, flat roofs were abandoned in favor of conventional pitched roofs.

These sixty buildings, all together, were designed to house twelve thousand people, though it is likely that quite a few more were crammed into them. In addition, the Soviets themselves supervised extensive construction of "temporary" dormitories to house construction workers and then factory workers. The construction of fifty two-story apartment buildings with wooden frames and stucco exteriors was ordered in the spring of 1931. In July an additional 150 dormitory units, one-story prefabricated structures, were begun. However, by October only twenty-eight of these apartment buildings and none of the dormitory units were ready for occupancy.[4] The dugouts covered with tenting that had been erected for the first winter were used again during the winter of 1932. Most of this housing lacked indoor plumbing and was not connected to the central heating system.

All these buildings were clustered in what were known as the Northern, Southern, Eastern, and Western settlements. These neighborhood names persisted until recently. Indeed, as happens in many countries, much of the "temporary" housing was used for many years. The last of these barracks was demolished in the early 1990s.

The utopian city plan of 1930 was overtaken by economic necessity. It was formally abandoned in 1932. In its stead there were dense clusters of low-rise housing, both temporary and permanent. The tree-filled parks, the broad avenues, the large stadium, and the imposing central square all disappeared from the official map.

Workers in the new automobile factory would live very much as industrial workers lived in all parts of the world: in families, and in crowded urban neighborhoods with both standard and substandard housing. Just a year earlier there had been a different vision for Russia's first modern city: it would transform human nature by means of clean and spacious neighborhoods filled with communal care and cultural opportunities. "The socialistic city," Allan Austin wrote in anticipation, "is giving to the Soviet Government a proving ground for its theories. Here they will fail or triumph."

These photos, taken from similar viewpoints, show evolution at the Worker's City. Allan took the photo at the top, "A general view, taken about June 15 '31." The fifteen apartment buildings comprising the second row line the horizon; fifteen more are hidden behind them. The scaffold towers were used to hoist building materials. The construction of a third row of buildings in taking place in the foreground. A fourth row was started two months later. Later that year another Austin engineer took the photo in the center. Here the fourth row is just emerging, and in the distance two-story wood-frame barracks are being erected. The Russian photo, at the bottom, taken in 1935, shows the third row of flat-roofed apartments that Austin designed (*left*) and the fourth-row apartments (*right*), which have more conventional pitched roofs. The park between these rows remains to this day. *Allan Austin Construction Album, The Austin Company Archives, GAZ Museum of History*

The Soviet government pressed on to complete the factory, devoted all available resources to that end, and triumphed. In the heat of that struggle the government chose to abandon plans for a "city of utopia." The first attempt to build a socialist city from the ground up, in order to uplift and to transform humanity, was not realized. This civic failure would influence the future of Soviet society.

During the spring of the year Allan grew homesick as he watched this vision fade. It had not been his personal vision, but he had struggled to realize it, and work on a visionary project was stimulating. Now the excitement waned, and the role of Austin engineers in the city project declined. Allan decided to return to America with his parents after their visit to Nizhny Novgorod in August.

Meanwhile, Margretta emerged from her doldrums with the most satisfying experience of her stay in Russia. A circus took up residence in downtown Nizhny Novgorod, including a horseman of some fame. Margretta engaged him for riding lessons. She was not an athletic person and had never before attempted to cultivate such a skill. Much to her surprise, the instructor insisted that she begin by riding bareback in the circus ring so she might learn the feel of the horse and develop control with her knees and her thighs. She told of this experience frequently: it was both frightening and exciting. She progressed through the summer to the point where she was allowed to try a saddle. Margretta had always relied upon her intellectual gifts—and upon her beauty. It broadened her sense of herself to master a physical skill as well.

In his final letter from Russia to his parents, Allan mentioned Margretta's horseback adventure. Clearly, however, he did not appreciate its significance to her.

June 22, 1931

Dearest Mother and Dad—

I have been doing very little writing recently because there has really been nothing to write about, good or bad. The job goes on, as usual, and so does the rest of our life here.

Our food from America has been shipped from Leningrad and is in transit here. Within a week we should have it. This will again make it possible to consider a trip to Kazan [a city down river from Nizhny Novgorod], and we shall probably go in a couple of weeks.

Margretta is still taking her riding lessons, and I guess is progressing very well. I haven't seen her ride but will probably do so this rest day.

Margretta's "graduation" photo from equestrian training in Nizhny Novgorod.
Margretta Austin Jamieson Album

ПРОИЗВОДСТВЕННО — БЫТОВАЯ
КОММУНА. ИМ. „13 ЛЕТ ОКТЯБРЯ"
АВТОЗАВОД—ЗАПАД.ПОСЁЛОК   19 $\frac{17}{IV}$ 31г.

Posed before their dormitory in the Western Settlement in 1931 are the members of an industrial commune named in honor of the thirteenth anniversary of the October revolution. *The Austin Company Archives*

We often hear strange expressions in our conversation here, and another funny one has just come along. Yesterday a couple of the [Russian] girls in our office had apparently taken some time off in the afternoon when they were supposed to be at work. Today at Noon, a mass meeting of all the office workers was called. When we asked an interpreter what it was all about she told us that the girls had committed a "social blemish." (So don't you commit any social blemishes, or the G.P.U. will get you!) However, a public reprimand of this sort is about the most drastic punishment used. If one has any Socialist convictions at all, it is the punishment most feared.

The Depression in the United States was deepening, hundreds of thousands of workers were being laid off from their jobs, and an equal number were forced to accept wage reductions. The Herbert Hoover administration did nothing useful. Labor agitation increased, and radical opinions flourished on both the Left and the Right. Some capitalists were eager to blame Russia and communist agitators for the troubles they had with their workers. Henry Ford was himself a leading "Red baiter," despite his huge role in the Autostroy project. But popular anxieties about Russia caused embarrassment to firms, like the Austin Company, that were doing business here. Allan continued his letter with a reflection on this problem.

A recent *Saturday Evening Post* carried a big story on forced labor in Russia. The facts were about as we see them, but the author's prejudice spoiled the whole story, which had no balance to it.

The recent increase in U.S. fear of Russia only helps European countries that want to secure Russia's orders and to limit U.S. participation in the business that Russia places. The recent trend has benefited Europe. Even France is on the verge of a trade agreement with Russia. Yesterday a large Italian delegation was here, coming right out to the job in their special train of five sleepers and a diner.

In my opinion, if anyone has to fear the menace of Russian supremacy and the spread of Socialism, it is the European countries. Already they have strong Socialist and even Communist minorities in their political ring, whereas we have none to speak of. Yet they are bagging every possible Russian order, supplying credit, etc., while we are timid about doing business with people who do some things that we disapprove of. I believe that there is sentiment here in favor of U.S. goods rather than European. But the constant babble against Russia from the U.S., and the Russians need to hunt for credit, leads them away from us.

We had our brick stove taken out of the sun room today, so we hope that summer will stay with us. I wanted to take a bath when I came home this evening, but the running water was as dark as water in a radiator. So I stayed dirty.

We want to know your plans for the summer. Mr. Bryant says you will never find a better time to take a vacation, for rubles are very cheap this year.

Allan

Allan soon learned that his parents, along with his brother and sister, did plan a return trip to Europe and on to Russia in August. Indeed there was no time for further correspondence to reach them in Cleveland. The Austins made their visit, and Allan and Margretta returned with them to Cleveland.

The only document remaining that concerns Allan Austin in Russia is his official letter of discharge from Austin Company employment, dated August 20, 1931. The letter reveals that Allan's salary had been eighty dollars a week, with a bonus for foreign work of $105 per month. He was furnished with $1,400 for transportation home to Cleveland. The document concluded with a stern paragraph just above signatures by Allan S. Austin and H. F. Miter. "The parties, hereto, for good and sufficient consideration hereby mutually release and discharge each other from all contracts, promises and agreements between them to the date hereof and agree that no contract of employment for any future time exists." Times were hard, and construction work was scarce. Wilbert Austin insisted that his son be treated just like any other junior engineer. It would be 1932 before another job was found for Allan at the Austin Company.

14

"FORTRESSES TAKEN BY BOLSHEVIKS"

The year 1931 saw an amazingly successful effort toward factory construction. In the spring of the year, however, important problems had to be resolved if this was to happen. Fred Coleman, the Austin Company engineer in charge of the installation of new equipment, raised the first problem in a letter to Autostroy.[1]

March 2, 1931

Gentlemen:

Equipment for the Plant is arriving; no place has been prepared for receiving or storing it; where it will go or what will be done with it is unknown. Equipment is arriving without any advance information or documents. The works [labels on the crates] indicate the building in which it will be installed, but it is not known who has shipped this equipment, where it comes from and what the cases contain.

When Fred Coleman sounded the alarm in March, snow drifted through the open roof of the Pressed Steel Building. Perhaps this vast space was used for equipment storage by June 20, when this panorama was photographed, even though clerestory windows remained to be installed. On July 26 a brigade of proud metalworkers posed to receive the Red Banner of Socialist Competition. *The Austin Company Archives*

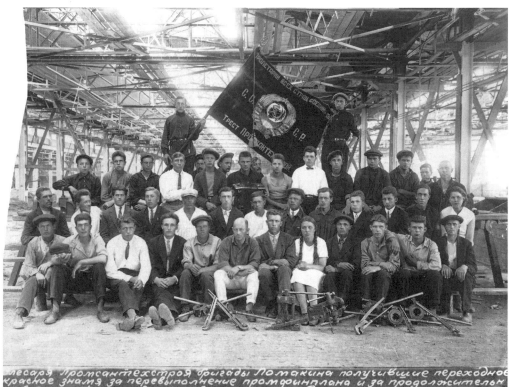

It was imperative to avoid the situation that had arisen the previous summer when shipments had been scattered about on the river bank and important pieces had been lost or stolen before new machinery could be assembled. Coleman proposed a single depot on the factory site for the storage of all equipment until it could be installed.

Two things have got to be done at once. The first is to prepare the Pressed Steel Building to receive the equipment. The second is to advise Moscow that they have got to cooperate and send complete information on all shipments, and do it before the equipment is received at Autostroy.

The work to be done at the Pressed Steel Building is to move the garage, to build track into the building, level and ground and plank it so that equipment can be stored there, not directly on the ground but with an air space beneath. The track just south of the building should be extended approximately 40 meters. The hoist should be erected together with the necessary platforms for handling equipment from the freight cars to the hoist.

The situation is serious. An emergency exists and no time should be lost in getting these things done. If this condition is not remedied promptly and vigorously, in 30 days the situation will be hopeless.
F. A. Coleman

Kurt Schultz in his essay, "Building the 'Soviet Detroit,'" described the larger picture of bureaucratic confusion as seen from Moscow.

In mid-February 1931, Vesenkha [the Supreme Council of the National Economy of the USSR] responded to the chaos by again reorganizing the chain of command at the factory, while the STO [Council of Labor and Defense] issued a detailed decree covering virtually every outstanding question of supply and future production. The decree gave VATO and Avtostroi until 1 April to calculate the total cost of bringing the factory on line and spelled out the obligations of every enterprise and bureau involved in construction. Although this was Moscow's strongest intervention to date, little came of it. A month later, *Za industrializatsiiu* [*For Industrialization*] reported that the STO decree remained "suspended in the stifling air of bureaucracy." VATO and Avtostroi were putting their final estimate together "at a snail's pace." In early March, officials from the trusts and factories responsible for supplying the automobile plant gathered to clarify delivery schedules and costs, but agreed to nothing. To be sure, an official of Vesenkha's Electro-Technical Association gleefully observed that with the STO decree in hand it was now possible to "grab some people by the throat and get everything we need for production." What he wanted, however, was 400,000 gold rubles to import machinery the association was supposed to produce itself.

In retrospect it is amazing that Avtostroi completed even the most critical shops and assembly lines by the 1 November deadline.[2]

Schultz's analysis ignores the role of the Austin Company, which proved to be decisive. However, before Austin could move construction forward with dispatch, a final crisis with Autostroy needed to be resolved. The problem erupted in April, about the time of the spring flood. The contracts between Autostroy and the Austin Company specified that all construction was to be carried forward "under the direct supervision" of the Austin Company and that "all orders . . . relating to the supervision of construction and installation of equipment must be fully carried out by AUTOSTROY or its contractors." A contract appendix executed on August 22, 1929, specified: "AUTOSTROY agrees not to engage any persons of the engineering and technical staff of the CONCERN [the Austin Company] delegated for the construction of the plant, and not to carry on any negotiations with the above mentioned persons to that effect without the consent of the CONCERN."[3]

Nevertheless on April 10, 1931, while Harry Miter, the project superintendent, was traveling from his Berlin vacation toward Nizhny Novgorod, Autostroy issued an order transferring several Austin Company engineers to the supervision of Autostroy. When Miter was presented with this order upon his return, he responded vigorously.[4]

April 19, 1931

AUTOSTROY
Nijni Novgorod
Gentlemen:

Your order No. 446, dated April 10th, refers to the assignment of part of our Engineers under the direct supervision of Autostroy, with the intention, apparently, to contract with these men direct. This arrangement is not in accordance with our Agreement with Autostroy and not satisfactory to us.

We have set up an organization of Engineering Specialists to function as a Unit and we cannot function on any other basis, both from a contract standpoint and for the best interests of the work still to be accomplished.

There is no objection to contracting with individual engineers on routine matters, but decisions of importance and all matters of construction and engineering problems must be referred to The Austin Company for decision and attention. Our responsibilities from a Company standpoint do not permit any deviation from this routine.

In order that there may be no further question with regard to this matter, we request that you immediately cancel the order No. 446, referred to above, and issue further instructions to all concerned in your organization and other organizations contracting with us, so that no misunderstanding can come up to handicap the progress of the work which after all is the ultimate desire of everyone concerned. . . .

H. F. Miter

The Soviets were eager to build strong engineering and administrative units of their own, and they were used to recruiting help from a trickle of radical European and American dissidents who visited Russia. They found some Austin Company engineers easier to deal with than others and these, they may have hoped, might be willing to work for Autostroy directly.

Surely none of the Austin Company engineers—conservative men with intense loyalties to their company—would have responded favorably to an Autostroy proposition. Miter was correct that the ability of the Austin Company to complete high-quality construction, faster than any other company

George Bryant's eyes revealed his steely determination, and all who worked with Bryant remember the look. *The Austin Company Archives*

in the world, depended upon very close coordination within a team of engineers and managers who were accustomed to working with one another. The team that the Austin Company had sent to Nizhny Novgorod was the best in the world—the "Olympic finalists" of industrial construction management. As Allan Austin had written, they came "with a strong sense of Austin spirit and ability . . . to serve the Russian people." No participant would willingly leave such a team in mid-game.

George A. Bryant, Jr., had accompanied Miter from Berlin to Nizhny Novgorod. Bryant had been promoted to general manager of the Austin Company; Wilbert Austin had reduced his own responsibilities for reasons of health. Bryant was a brilliant manager. It appears that, given the attempt by Autostroy to reorganize the administration of construction during this critical year, Bryant had decided to remain in Russia to push the project along. Unlike Harry Miter, whose frequent letters of complaint might suggest fatigue or weakness, George Bryant had boundless self-confidence and a determined gaze that might have stared down, if necessary, even a Joseph Stalin.

While Harry Miter chided Autostroy leadership in Nizhny Novgorod for their attempt to recruit Austin Company personnel, George Bryant returned to Moscow to make the same point to more senior officials. He was apparently successful, for he wrote to his wife Edith on April 21, "You remember the last meetings you witnessed here? Well, we are getting along better now." He also told her that the construction job "is going good in some parts. Some of our old men are doing fine, some are not so hot. We'll get it going better shortly."[5]

Once George Bryant took matters in hand, no more letters of complaint passed between the Austin Company and Autostroy. Indeed, a month later, nine Soviet officials from the construction site were placed on trial in Nizhny Novgorod for willful neglect and suppression of forty-two recommendations submitted by American specialists on the job. The new Labor Palace where the trial was conducted could seat three thousand people, and it was filled beyond its capacity. An American reporter wrote, "The workers rightly regarded the trial as an attack on bureaucracy because not only the suggestions of Americans and other foreign specialists, but those of Russian workers also have been buried in red tape. . . . The court established the fact that the factory officials received, and in many cases approved, foreign or native suggestions, but that nothing had been done to put them in effect."[6]

When reporter Milly Bennett arrived in June, she found Bryant in the construction office, looking very much in charge.

In the split log field office from which he has been directing the Nizhni project, he sits talking easily, readily. . . . Bryant is an American combination of successful engineer and big business executive. A tall man, easy and athletic in his movements, whose gray tweeds are well pressed, he is self-assured and quick to give orders that he expects to have obeyed without question.

He is a fearless fellow, for he's been telling the Communists right along that good, honest, efficient work, not politics, builds mammoth auto plants and workers' cities. In common with most Americans, Bryant dislikes politics. He never sees them the way the Russians do, as the bread and wine of a new life.

Bennett found Autostroy officials still defensive about their attempt to hire engineers away from the Austin Company.

Stephen Dybetz, chief of work for Avtostroi (the State Automobile Construction Trust), says: "It has been difficult for American engineers to adapt themselves to Russian psychology and conditions. Russia has to have American specialists. For automobile construction, for machinery and metallurgy—we must hire individual foreign specialists and work right with them. The American engineer, to work successfully in Russia, must be part of the Soviet organization, working in Soviet offices alongside Soviet engineers. To be really useful, he must be ready at any moment to be shifted to any job where he is needed. You can't move a firm from job to job."

And Bryant says: "When the Soviet Union purchases a plan from a firm which has had to go through hard experience to attain its reputation, such a firm is bound to send over a competent force to handle the project. If dozens of individuals are hired, they may be competent men, but they are not accustomed to working together. They don't 'mesh.' A firm sends out a complete unit which functions like a football team."

This factory panorama was photographed in 1935 when landscaping was in place. On the far left are the offices, trade school, and dining facilities. The façade of the Pressed Steel Building, where auto body parts were stamped, has a smokestack directly in front of it. The front of the assembly line building faces the camera. To the right are three buildings with compound roofs to vent heat and fumes: the first is the shop where springs were manufactured; the second and third are forge shops where engine blocks were stamped. The foundry, where molten metal was poured, is behind these and cannot be seen. The central power plant, not built under The Austin Company's supervision, rises on the horizon. All the factory buildings were substantially completed by November 1931. *GAZ Museum of History*

Work on the many factory buildings now moved more swiftly. Late in June George Bryant headed homeward. Early in July, P. Ya. Makarovsky, Allan Austin's friend who was now chief engineer in the VATO construction department, reported that the deplorable situation at the construction site was indeed improving, as were relationships between Austin, Autostroy, and other Soviet partners.[7]

Not only did Miter's letters of complaint cease, but after June, Allan Austin's correspondence with his father also ceased, closing our two most intimate windows into the construction process. Fortunately Philip K. Davis, another Austin Company engineer, wrote additional recollections.[9]

As the job progressed the work was modernized as far as possible. At the dock, materials were unloaded by power cranes, conveyors and skip hoists directly from the barges to railroad cars. Two central gravel washing and concrete mixing plants were installed, with a total capacity of 1100 cubic yards per day, from which ready mixed concrete was hauled in dump trucks to all sections of the job. One of these plants was equipped to produce heated concrete for winter work. All buildings were equipped with material hoists. American-made crawler cranes were used in the erection of the 14,000 tons of structural steel. These machines, equipped with various excavating attachments, were used for general and sewer trench excavation. A locomotive crane also aided in unloading and distributing materials. Approximately fifty miles of standard gauge railroad track provided facilities for transporting materials from the main Nijni-Novgorod line, the dock, and the various auxiliary material plants. During the year 1931, fifteen locomotives, 290 freight cars and 125 automobile trucks were used for all long hauls on the site.

Even with this extensive transportation system the peasant horse with hand-made wagon was required to transport a large quantity of materials. During the peak of the last season 5,000 horses were used.

The magnitude of the project necessitated the construction of a large number of temporary manufacturing plants to produce the numerous construction materials which [in the United States] are ordinarily delivered to the job site completely manufactured. The job saw-mill and planing-mill would have been well suited to the requirements of a large city. They were completely equipped with all the necessary modern machinery for the manufacture of sized lumber—sash, doors, and other items of interior wood finish from the logs as delivered from the forest.

At the mechanical yard were shops for the manufacture of various metal building-products, also for the manufacture and repair of construction tools and equipment. . . . Operation on a 24-hour day basis by inexperienced operators demanded more than the equipment was able to stand.

With the exception of structural steel and steel sash material, all construction materials used on this project were produced within the boundaries of the USSR. . . .

To complete the construction in the time allotted would require several thousand workers in the United States; in Russia this should be multiplied by four or five [because workers and supervisors were inexperienced, power equipment was scarce, and work rules were awkward]. During the year 1930, an average of 16,000 people were registered on the payrolls, and during 1931, the maximum of 40,000 was reached. . . . Approximately forty per cent of the laborers on the Nijni auto plant were women.[7]

183

Six enormous factory buildings and a dozen offices, schools, and support facilities were being rushed to completion simultaneously. For the laborers on the job, their Russian supervisors, and the American engineers who orchestrated the integration of the effort, this was the most awesome human construction they had beheld. The emergence of the buildings themselves and the obvious necessity to complete them before winter would have provided every group with ample incentive to lay aside differences and pull together. Through the long summer days, laborers undoubtedly worked far longer than the regulation eight hours, while their supervisors and the visiting Americans worked along with them. Sergo Ordzhonikidze, the new chairman of the Supreme Council of the National Economy (VSNH), visited the site on September 10, and after his departure work proceeded even more furiously.[9]

As particular buildings were completed in September and October, installation of machinery and amassing of supplies for production became top priorities. The previous April the Soviets had purchased from the Ford Motor Company, for $3.4 million, the machinery, tools, dies, jigs, and fixtures for the manufacture of the Model A sedan and the Model AA truck. Ford was eager to ship this equipment, since it was converting its assembly line to manufacture the new Ford V-8.

Reporter Boris Agapov visited the construction site in September and later wrote with typical caustic wit.[10]

Right now, checking resources before opening the plant, managers beat their brains over these problems:
— Are we able to procure materials in time?
— Are we able to deliver and to store them?
— Are we able to inventory the raw materials and finished materials on hand?

Agapov noted that some shops were in production already. The woodworking shop had been making body parts for the assembly plant in downtown Nizhny Novgorod. The forge shop and the tool shop were complete and ready to produce, but chaos in the procurement of supplies undermined their efforts.

Breakdown in woodworking shop: no timber, no forgings.

Why are there no forgings?

Because the machine repair shop does not provide them.

I go to the machine repair shop to find out the problem.

—Why no forgings?

—The forge shop doesn't provide them.

I inquire at the forge shop: "Why?"

—No iron.

—But why? . . .

—The procurement department. . . etc., etc.

What does it all mean, comrades, I ask? A new plant—and the same old songs.

"There are no such fortresses that cannot be taken by Bolsheviks." So read the banner encircling the globe display erected in front of the Assembly Building for the November 2, 1931, celebration of the factory's completion. *GAZ Museum of History*

On November 1, one month ahead of schedule, the Austin Company presented the finished factory to Autostroy. Autostroy gave the Austin Company a formal letter of acceptance. A large public celebration was held on November 2, 1931. Austin Company engineers departed during the month of November, the last leaving on December 1. The final payment for Austin Company services, due on that date, was received.

Was construction actually finished? Victor Reuther, who worked in the factory two years later, told the author that when he arrived doors were missing from some buildings, allowing winter winds to whip through. Yet he felt that the Austin Company had substantially completed its task.

Indeed, both Austin and Autostroy were motivated to "declare victory and go home." Once construction was officially completed, Autostroy could relinquish its responsibility to other agencies, and the Austin engineers could begin their homeward journeys before winter set in. In the manic pace of the Five Year Plan it was unthinkable to allow a project to drag beyond the designated completion date, though it was common for swift work to be shoddy and, in fact, incomplete. It is unlikely that work performed under Austin Company supervision was shoddy. Yet some structural elements may have been missing because Autostroy could not get materials to the site before the deadline—or, at the Worker's City, because apartments were occupied prematurely.

In the United States, neither the Austin Company nor the client would have considered a job completed with many details unattended to. However, if the Russian client, Autostroy, wished to declare completion of this extraordinarily difficult effort—a month ahead of schedule!—Austin engineers were happy to accept this decision and depart.

"It was strange," Allan Austin would recall years later. "There weren't any continuing associations or correspondence. One reason was that the Russians were fearful of becoming personally friendly with us lest they be accused of being tainted with Capitalism. So when we left it was like dropping a curtain behind us."[11]

15

"THE USSR AT THE WHEEL"

On January 1, 1932, the Soviets officially opened the Nizhny Novgorod automobile factory. In the Associated Press article that announced this event to the world, the fervor of the celebration was caught in the words of one speaker: "When we place the USSR at the wheel of an automobile and a *muzhik* (peasant) on a tractor, let the venerable capitalists boasting of their 'civilization' try to reach us."

The Associated Press article indicated further that the total cost of factory, machinery, and Worker's City had reached $119,000,000. The factory was designed to produce 144,000 vehicles annually: 94,000 light trucks and 50,000 passenger cars. Ford Motor Company technicians, present to assist the start of production, replaced Austin Company engineers in the American Village. For the first quarter of 1932, production would begin slowly, with an emphasis upon mastering techniques and upon manufacturing tools, dies, and automotive components. Only seven hundred vehicles were scheduled to be completed for that quarter.

However, even this modest schedule proved a challenge. Recruiting skilled workers, and then retaining them, continued to be difficult. Autostroy had sent about 230 workers and engineers to study at Ford Motor Company facilities in the United States, but upon their return some of these were assigned to other plants. Efforts to recruit skilled workers from other factories were often unsuccessful: either workers with relevant skills did not exist, or factory managers would not release them despite orders from Moscow to do so.[1]

To further complicate matters, local Communist Party and union leadership took control of production and ignored the guidance of resident engineers. By March the situation was so chaotic that two members of the Politburo were dispatched by Joseph Stalin to investigate. The *New York Times* reported on April 4, 1932:

MASS OUTPUT FAILS

SOVIET PLANT HALTS

LABOR TO BE CURBED.[2]

Production has been held up at the huge new Nizhni-Novgorod automobile plant and two of Joseph Stalin's closest associates in the Political Bureau of the Communist party, L. M. Kaganovich and Commissar of Heavy Industry Ordjonikidze, were sent there to find the reasons.

The Soviet Government has begun to realize that the efficient running of modern mass production plants requires bosses with authority and obedience and discipline in the lower ranks. Ever since Joseph Stalin's speech last March about improving the status of engineers there has been a struggle to increase the authority of factory managers and technical personnel. . . .

The findings of MM. Kaganovich and Ordjonikidze are summed up in a slashing manifesto which the Central Committee of the Communist party published today blaming the Nizhni-Novgorod Communist and labor union organizations in no unmeasured terms for mismanagement, interference with and infraction of the "party line" and "slander of the engineering and technical personnel." . . .

The secretary of the regional party committee at Nizhni-Novgorod was ordered dismissed. The plant's foundry and assembly captains were ordered discharged. . . . Resumption of operation in time to complete the program for the first six months of 1932 on schedule was demanded.

In 1932 the city of Nizhny Novgorod was renamed "Gorky," after its native son, Maxim Gorky, the greatest writer of the revolutionary era. This name was retained until 1991. Henceforth the factory would be known—first informally and later officially—as GAZ, the acronym for Gorky Automobile Factory.

According to the *Wall Street Journal,* Soviet automobile production reached 25,500 in 1932, and 47,700 in 1933. Most of this production came from GAZ. These figures represented only a fraction of the capacity that the factory was designed for, and a significant portion of this production involved merely the assembly of Model A kits purchased from the Ford Motor Company in America.

In the final days of 1933, Walter Reuther and his brother Victor arrived in Gorky, made their way to the American Village, and were hired at GAZ. Walter Reuther would later organize the United Auto Workers (UAW) of America. His influence upon the automobile industry was to be second only to that of Henry Ford himself. The Reuther brothers' year at GAZ was important to their personal and their political development.

Walter Reuther began work in America as a tool and die maker at the Ford plant that produced the Model A. He was promoted to foreman. Even from that management position, Reuther encouraged workers to join the communist-led union that was organizing strikes against Depression-era wage cuts— strikes that included the attack on the Ford facility described in chapter 3. In 1933, in a purge of labor union sympathizers, Reuther was fired. Walter and Victor then gathered their slim savings to finance an around-the-world tour of labor conditions in automobile factories.

The GAZ plant needed Walter Reuther's skills in tool and die making, and Victor's gifts as a translator. When they began work, Victor Reuther recalled, "The only heat in the whole building was in the small heat treatment department where metals were tempered. Otherwise temperatures were 30 to 35 degrees below zero [Fahrenheit] at the workbench. We found those early weeks very difficult."[3] But Walter was stimulated by the vitality of the enterprise and by the camaraderie at the "Red Corner" social and political center. He shared his enthusiasm in one of many letters to the English-language *Moscow Daily News.*

I have always pictured the Soviet Union as a beehive of social and industrial activity, but it was not until I arrived that I realized that even in my most imaginative moments I had underestimated the scope of Socialist construction. . . .

There are so many striking things here: the Red Corner, shop library, the numerous shop meetings where serious problems are discussed, the

Victor and Walter Reuther arrive at the American Village. Behind them stands the building where Allan and Margretta once lived. *Archives of Walter and Victor Reuther*

frank criticism exchanged between workers and the administration, and the multiplicity of cultural activities connected with shop life.

All these things are foreign to me as one who has received his training in a capitalist auto plant.

Reuther also concluded, however, that the tool and die operation was poorly organized. He made a great many suggestions for improvements in the spirit of "frank criticism" that he had observed. When most of his recommendations were ignored, Reuther bypassed the plant administration and wrote detailed letters for publication in the *Moscow Daily News*.

> The shortcomings responsible for the greater percentage of inefficiency in the Gorki Auto Plant are administrative in character. . . .
>
> Let us take the question of the monthly program. On the first of the month our department is given a list of dies that it has to construct, but the blue prints, castings and steel with which to construct the dies may be received any time from a week to two weeks later. As a result of this "system" the first half of the month sees inefficient work and the second half a mad rush to complete the program with quality being sacrificed. Instead of trying to build dies on a distinct monthly basis why not stagger the program so that there is a constant flow of new work into the shop and a steady flow of finished dies out. . . .
>
> Disregarding safety measures is another matter reflecting on administrative laxity. In our department, for example, heavy dies and castings are moved by a heavy crane. In every efficiently organized shop, safety holes are drilled in heavy dies and castings to allow for the use of lifting hooks. I could not find a single die in which these holes had been drilled.
>
> What was the result? I watched a crane man and two hook-up men trying to put a heavy casting on a machine; they struggled for an hour trying to get the casting to balance on the cable. Several times it slipped and fell to the floor. At last they hoped it would stay balanced and held their breath as they watched the crane man swing the casting over towards the machine.
>
> As the casting swung over the edge of the machine, the jerk of the crane stopping threw the casting off balance and it came crashing down on the machine, and as the machine man jumped aside to safety, the casting fell to the floor. It might have cost thousands of rubles had the casting fallen on the vital parts of a delicate machine, or it might have cost a life. Two rubles at the most would have been the cost of putting safety holes in this particular casting.

Reuther's letters were noticed in Moscow, and the Communist Party ordered GAZ management to implement many of his recommendations. This did not make Reuther popular among local managers, but both Walter and

Victor were admired by their fellow workers as they pushed to make the plant safer and more efficient. Walter was proclaimed a Stakhanovite, a "Hero of Production," and he was assigned to lead a sixteen-man shock brigade.

There was an amusing incident when the neighboring brake-drum department challenged Reuther's tool room to a "socialist competition" to "elevate the cultural level of the workers." The brake-drum division took the lead by decorating its workspace with artificial palm trees. Reuther reported:

> Well, we were put to shame in our department. . . . We put our heads together and decided that, gee, if we could just get some metal spoons for the cafeteria, so that when we ate the soup and *kasha* [porridge] we didn't have to use old wooden peasant spoons, it would be a symbol of cultural progress. We decided to build a die to stamp soup spoons out of scrap fender metal. We ran off enough for the whole department, and there was a great celebration when we took these up to the cafeteria. The brass band was out, and special banners were made and speeches were delivered that this marked another significant step forward in raising the cultural level.
>
> The next day there wasn't a damn spoon in sight. They'd all taken them home with them. There was a big meeting, with protests made about stealing state property. Henceforth a new procedure applied. One would enter the cafeteria, surrender his factory pass which had his picture on it, and he would get a soup spoon. Going out you would return the soup spoon and get your pass back.
>
> We won the Socialist competition.

By the end of 1934, a year after the Reuthers' arrival, there were significant improvements. The factory was now heated. Walter Reuther won a battle to equip tool room workers with aprons to prevent their baggy clothing from getting snagged in the machines. When Reuther arrived it had taken seven months to produce a single stamp or die; now Russian labor was turning out three and four dies a month.

There were other changes as well. In response to the rise of Adolf Hitler, Reuther's department at GAZ began secret tooling for army tanks. Late in 1934 Stalin's paranoid search for saboteurs began—purges that by the end of the decade would claim millions of victims. Walter Reuther remembered tearful

The palm trees introduced by the brake-drum department suggested a happy workplace. *Archives of Walter and Victor Reuther*

Workers study the operations of a large press. *Archives of Walter and Victor Reuther*

women and children appearing in the cafeteria without their husband and father. "The others in the dining hall knew that any gesture of comfort to the stricken family, even just asking them what had happened, would be interpreted as sympathy, and they might well be the next victims just because of such a gesture." Victor Reuther recalled a late-night knock on their neighbor's door. "He was an Italian political immigrant and married a young Russian woman. I worked with him every day on the bench. The knock on the door came at three o'clock in the morning. We opened the door to see what was going on. The secret police came and arrested him—took him away. No explanation was given to his Russian wife. There was no trial, and nothing was ever head of him again."

In the spring of 1935 the Reuthers left the plant to continue their journey around the world. Walter would later summarize their experience: "We were enthused over the eagerness of the workers to learn technique. They were in a new world, building factories and machines. But we were disillusioned by the workings of bureaucracy. There was a tremendous power down below, on the workers' level—lots of pioneer enthusiasm. But the power of the state inter-fered. Vic and I had American passports and could leave. Unless you've been there, you don't fully appreciate what it means to have to stay."

This Russian experience influenced Walter Reuther's career. His dedica-tion to automobile workers was deepened. When he returned to the United States, he helped to organize the United Auto Workers and also the Congress of Industrial Organizations (CIO). Following the Second World War, under Reuther's leadership, American auto workers made themselves the best-paid assembly-line workers in the world.

Reuther's Russian experience also convinced him that communism could not contribute to the welfare of American workers. He worked to build a genu-inely democratic labor union movement with a practical agenda of worker benefits rather than a political agenda set by theoreticians. Reuther worked hard to keep communists out of leadership in the UAW, the CIO, and the American labor movement in general.

Production problems at GAZ were gradually overcome. Russian engineers made improvements to the Model A cars and Model AA trucks so they might be more durable for rough roads and harsh winters. In the later 1930s, larger truck models were developed for the needs of collective farms and the mili-tary. The factory also manufactured a line of light tanks.

In August 1939 George Bryant and Harry Miter returned to Gorky to see the progress made. "We were dumbfounded," Miter wrote home on August 30. "Workers City has been tremendously increased . . . 120,000 people . . . new apartments are 6 to 8 stories . . . paved streets . . . quite a few flowers . . . people look better."[4] Two days later Hitler attacked Poland. Bryant and Miter decided to flee homeward; and since Russia and Germany were not yet at war, they were able secure seats on a flight from Moscow to Berlin. From there they took a train to Switzerland.

The Great Patriotic War, as Russians refer to their theater of the World War II, may prove to be the most exciting chapter in the history of GAZ when all the facts are known. Victor Reuther recently expressed this opinion: "If Rus-sians hadn't had the Gorky Autoplant they may not have won the war. It was critical to military defense production."[5] This is also an important chapter in Soviet-American cooperation. The author has been moved by anecdotes of

Ninety-four-year-old Victor Reuther greeted Natalia Kolesnikova, director of the GAZ Museum of History, while Galina Moleva of the GAZ marketing department looked on, May 4, 2000. "I want the story to be told," Reuther said. "It is a great contribution by workers and management from outside to help Russia at a critical time in her history. The Austin family helped the Russians to have faith in their own ability to overcome problems." *GAZ Museum of History*

the period and by the recollections of two veteran workers who lived though the conflict. Formal research into this period, from a post–Cold War perspective, remains to be undertaken.

Of the three principal allies—Great Britain, Russia, and the United States—who eventually defeated Adolf Hitler and the Axis powers, Russia bore the heaviest burden. Only Russia had its soil invaded by German armies, and Russian combat losses were far greater than those of its allies. The Soviets' determined and costly defenses of Leningrad, Moscow, and Stalingrad turned the tide of the war in the East and—by pinning down vast German armies—made it possible for England and the United States to invade Italy successfully, and then France.

"Have you ever experienced bombing?" Sergei Ivanovich Vlasov asked the author and other visiting Americans in September 1999. We admitted that we had not. "I hope you never do," he continued, and then the venerable autoworker told of his experience. German bombing raids on GAZ began on July 4, 1943.[6]

During the war we stayed at the factory. We were not allowed to go home. We ate there and we slept there. German aircraft usually arrived at a few minutes before midnight. They dropped illuminating flares. Every aircraft had a mission to destroy some part of the plant.

The Germans had a detailed layout of the factory because a German engineer had helped to lay out the communications at the plant. He left GAZ in 1939 and later he guided the bombing. Because they knew the layout of the plant, the Germans could bomb methodically. First they attacked the main assembly line and adjacent buildings. Fighters came over to destroy the anti-aircraft installations on the roofs, and the crews that manned them were killed. Then bombers arrived. We saw the main assembly building being bombed. When the Germans dropped incendiary bombs, workers stationed on the roof were assigned to put out the fires. But the roof collapsed and they were killed as well.

I was assistant manager of the plant production shop. On the roof of our shop there were four points with anti-aircraft machine guns and cannons. When we came under attack, the manager of our shop thought that it would be useless to require people to stay on the roof. So we ordered everyone to go down to the basement and shelter under the foundations of the big presses. We knew that we could repair equipment, but you can't restore people.

Because we saved people, on the third day following the bombing of our building we were able to resume production of parts such as wheels for artillery and shells for Katyusha rockets. There was no roof, nor windows, only columns.

The whole factory was restored to production within 100 days.

Most of the damaged factory buildings were rebuilt on their original foundations. Only a few walls built under Austin Company supervision remain standing to this day, and some buildings, such as the main assembly building, have been expanded by the addition of new levels. Still, the general layout of the automobile plant remains strikingly similar to the original design.

Factory officials recalled that two-thirds of Russia's trucks were manufactured at GAZ, but because of enormous losses in combat, all of Russia's factories together could produce only one-third of the trucks required during the war years. Most of the trucks needed to support the Russian war effort were supplied by the American Lend-Lease program, and many of these were assembled at GAZ.

The shipping crates in the background (*top left*) contain knocked-down American trucks that arrived at GAZ on railroad flatcars. Workers in the foreground break open a crate to expose a truck frame with the engine, drive train, and wheels attached. Subsequent photos show stages of reassembly. The work was done outdoors because the damaged factory was crowded with Russia's own production. *GAZ Museum of History*

The American public was unwilling to enter the war directly until Pearl Harbor was bombed by the Japanese on December 7, 1941. Prior to that, however, President Franklin Roosevelt persuaded Congress to approve an innovative program to supply war material to the Allies. America had a huge manufacturing capacity, which the president realized must be converted to war production. Roosevelt won popular support for his program with a simple analogy: "Suppose my neighbor's house catches fire, and I have a length of garden hose. . . ." By law the equipment could only be "loaned" or "leased," but in fact no payment was expected, and no return was anticipated.

Hitler invaded Russia on June 22, 1941. Two days later Roosevelt announced the first Lend-Lease shipments to Russia. Shipments went to Murmansk in the north, a dangerous route through U-boat–infested waters. More shipments took the longer but safer journey through the Persian Gulf to Iran and then north into Russia by train.

Of the tens of thousands of American truck kits that reached GAZ, a large proportion were Studebaker trucks. In 1998 a retired Russian worker told this author that following the war, he was part of delegation that visited South Bend, Indiana, in order to thank the Studebaker Company and its workers.

Following the war, GAZ produced a wide variety of trucks and cars of Russian design. Soviet authorities continued to stress high production volume, often at the expense of quality. During the 1950s and the 1960s, American car companies were also producing high volumes of automobiles that had appealing designs but required frequent repairs. When in the 1970s the Japanese began flooding the American market with cars that were more efficient, more durable, and less expensive, American manufacturers lost part of their market. They had to learn over again how to engineer and manufacture vehicles with long lives and few defects. Russian manufacturers did not encounter such competition until the collapse of communism and the opening of markets in the 1990s.

16

GAZELLE

The end of the Cold War created economic dislocation in Gorky, a center for Soviet defense industries, yet free market opportunities stimulated hope as well. In 1991 the city reclaimed its historic name, Nizhny Novgorod, and local industries moved toward privatization more swiftly than those in other Russian regions.

Nikolai Pugin, minister for the automotive industry under the Soviets, gathered a team of investigators to acquire the Gorky Automobile Plant from the new Russian state. The huge factory was reorganized as a joint-stock company called GAZ—an acronym for Gorky Automobile Plant. Pugin led GAZ for a decade and was regarded by his peers as one of the most capable industrial managers in Russia.

GAZ manufactured the Volga line of automobiles and was also Russia's principal producer of heavy trucks for the military and for collective farms. However, with the end of the Cold War and the collapse of communism there was little market for such large trucks. Automobile sales also declined when restrictions on the importation of used automobiles from Western Europe

Nikolai Pugin, once a Soviet bureaucrat, held the workers of GAZ together as the nation moved toward a market economy. *GAZ Museum of History*

were eased. Many Russians chose these used cars rather than a new Volga. All Russian-made automobiles were, in the opinion of an American analyst, "outdated, substandard, and unsafe."[1]

Nevertheless, Pugin was able to secure financing from the Russian government to modernize production lines at GAZ, and he established dealerships throughout Russia. In 1994 GAZ introduced a light commercial vehicle, the Gazelle, which quickly became both popular and profitable. Sold in a range of truck, van, and passenger configurations, the Gazelle—along with the smaller Sobol van that followed a few years later—met needs in the privatizing economy that no other manufacturer was attempting to supply.

During the second half of the 1990s GAZ produced more than 100,000 passenger cars each year, about 13 percent of Russia's output. In the face of both domestic and foreign competition, however, these cars were not profit-

This image from the front cover of a GAZ annual report conveys the excitement surrounding the 1994 introduction of the Gazelle. These vans and light trucks gave the factory a new lease on life. At right is the emblem that appears on GAZ vehicles. *GAZ Museum of History*

able for the company. GAZ also produced about 100,000 trucks and vans each year, half of Russia's capacity; this market proved quite profitable. Developing competitive, viable products and avoiding heavy losses made GAZ unique among vehicle manufacturers in the new Russia.

To raise quality to world standards, Pugin initiated a strategy reminiscent of the factory's founding collaborations with the Austin Company and the Ford Motor Company. In 1996 Pugin secured a $65 million loan from Russia's Avtobank. The funds were used to modernize facilities in preparation for a new car model, the Volga 3111. The largest new investment was a paint shop, erected by U.S. firm Haden International, which remains the finest auto finishing facility in Russia.

In January 1998 Pugin announced a joint venture with Fiat of Italy for the production of two Fiat models in Russia to be sold in the Russian market as soon as economic conditions might permit. The European Bank for Reconstruction and Development agreed to invest up to $70 million for a 20 percent share, and it assembled a banking syndicate to supply an additional $800 million. The agreement stipulated that 70 percent of the components for these automobiles would be manufactured in Russia. Production would begin with 15,000 Russian Fiats a year and increase as the market permitted, up to 75,000 vehicles. Later, Russian economic setbacks postponed implementation of this agreement.

To produce 250,000 vehicles in 1998, GAZ employed 105,000 workers. By Western standards this is an extraordinarily inefficient ratio of workers to output, reminiscent of the giant construction crews of 1931. However, more than half of these GAZ employees worked in apartment blocks, hospitals, kindergartens, and recreation facilities. The privatized company had inherited Soviet-style services that embraced not simply the factory but the whole surrounding "model city" of civil infrastructure and services begun seventy years earlier. Elsewhere in Nizhny Novgorod factories had closed and their neighborhoods languished. Pugin won the respect and affection of his employees by retaining the entire GAZ workforce in both factory and community and by continuing pension benefits for retirees.

By July 1998, when I made my first visit to Nizhny Novgorod, sustaining production and employment had become an extraordinarily difficult task. Russia—encouraged by Western advisers—raced toward capitalism without a credible banking system, without adequate tax collection, and without a legal system capable of enforcing contracts and curbing criminal conspiracies. Money, including much of the aid from the West, fled the country. (After my return home, when I received credit card bills for hotels, restaurants, and shopping, I observed that every charge had been processed through some offshore Caribbean bank. Since no company kept this money in Russia, the nation had received little economic benefit from my expenditures.)

Under the inefficient "command economy" of the Soviet era, Pugin and other Russian managers had developed techniques to bypass obstacles and to sustain production. Back-channel bartering of goods and services among industries was a survival strategy during the Communist era. Now in this strange new capitalism-without-money economy sophisticated barter networks were again employed.

I was told informally that up to 80 percent of the GAZ production was distributed through barter arrangements; automobiles and trucks were exchanged for manufacturing components, fuel, electricity, and a full range of

Сборка «черного» цельнометаллического кузова ГАЗ-2705 с использованием роботов

Nikolai Pugin obtained sufficient capital to automate portions of the Gazelle assembly line. Some other areas remained labor intensive. *GAZ Museum of History*

materials and services. Complex barter arrangements might require goods to pass through several hands; transactions might even be managed by intermediaries who harvested profits along the way. Lacking cash, GAZ might accept inferior parts or materials. Barter eliminated the economic "multiplier" effect that bank deposits, wages, purchases, and other cash transactions generate in a free economy; yet barter kept workers on the job and provided outlets for the vehicles that poured from the assembly line.

Throughout the summer of 1998 workers at GAZ were not paid, yet they came to work daily. The assembly line that I visited was busy and neat and clean; many women working the line wore crisp white blouses and earrings. Workers continued to receive housing, medical care, and a large subsidized meal at the factory. They lived in a crowded but modern urban community where heat, electricity, public transportation, and other services continued to function. Familiar routines of work and recreation persisted. Elsewhere in the city factories stood idle. The people at GAZ with whom I spoke, employees and retirees alike, had nothing but good words for Nikolai Pugin.

A few weeks after I departed, the cash-starved Russian economy took a dive: foreign debt payments were defaulted on and the ruble tumbled. Surprisingly, this economic crisis had a positive impact on demand for autos and light trucks. Russians could no longer afford imports from Western Europe, whether new or used, so the production of cars, trucks, and vans at the venerable factory increased. When I returned in September 1999 employees were being paid. The value of the rubles they received had declined, however; a Westerner might calculate typical GAZ wages at $100 a month, substantially lower than before. Yet from a worker's perspective rubles paid were superior to rubles withheld. Production was increasing and new models were under development. Employees boasted of management's long-range plans and aspirations. Hope survived.

However, following the devaluation of the ruble, GAZ could no longer make payments on the tens of millions of dollars it owed to creditors. Ten percent of GAZ shares had to be deposited with Avtobank as collateral for that outstanding loan. Pugin began negotiations with the European Bank for Reconstruction and Development toward a debt-for-equity swap that might transfer 30–40 percent of GAZ shares to the bank. But in the autumn of 2000 Pugin's delicate balancing act tipped over. Russian's new president, Vladimir Putin, undertook initiatives to reduce corruption, improve tax collection, and require businesses to replace obscure barter exchanges with more transparent money transactions. That October Russian federal tax collectors decreed that GAZ must pay $22 million in back taxes and $10 million in penalties over the next five years.

A few weeks later the Siberian Aluminum Group (SibAl), headed by Oleg Deripaska, announced that it had acquired 25 percent of GAZ stock. Deripaska is the youngest and one of the most successful, and most notorious, of Russia's new capitalist "oligarchs." By his twenty-fifth birthday he had employed brains, political connections, and rough tactics to gain control of 70 percent of Russia's huge and profitable aluminum industry. "In the bleak Siberian towns where the metal is produced," Christian Caryl observed in *Newsweek,* "contract killings were the order of the day."[2] The United States became sufficiently alarmed to deny Deripaska a visa.

Siberian Aluminum announced that it planned to take control of the vehicle manufacturer, and henceforth GAZ would have to operate on a cash basis. Many of the dealers who retail cars and trucks were unprepared to pay

The Volga 3111 at the Cleveland Auto Show, March 2001. Despite elaborate preparations, commercial production of this vehicle did not commence before new management cancelled the project in 2003. *Western Reserve Historical Society*

cash for GAZ vehicles, so they cancelled their orders. New cash requirements also disrupted some companies that supplied components to GAZ. The principal manufacturer of motors for GAZ vehicles, Zavolshye Engine Plant, shut down at the beginning of December because its electricity had been cut off for failure to pay bills. Lacking both engines and orders, Nikolai Pugin shut down the GAZ assembly lines on Thursday, December 7, 2000.

Victor Belyayev, a young executive from Siberian Aluminum, took charge. A week later he reopened the factory with a reduced assembly schedule. Thirty percent of GAZ employees were laid off, though GAZ continued to pay them two-thirds of their modest salaries. Senior managers, except for Pugin, were replaced by a team from SibAl. A new slogan was posted throughout the factory: "Our Wages Are Paid by Our Customers."

A special stockholders' meeting convened on January 20, 2001, to elect a new board of directors. Nikolai Pugin, now removed from daily management, retained the title of president and duties in "strategic and foreign economic development." One task was to protect the yet-to-be-implemented joint venture with Fiat. Also, his presence might help to sustain morale in the GAZ community.

The mayor of Nizhny Novgorod, Yuri Lebedev, was among those appointed to the new board of directors. He proposed taking the entire social sector of the GAZ enterprise—hospitals, educational facilities, housing, etc.—under municipal jurisdiction in order to reduce the burden on the company. This could be achieved if the city received new financial assistance from the federal (national) budget. Apparently such aid was forthcoming, for GAZ began to transfer these assets to the city during 2001.

The company was reorganized. Purchasing was spun off to one separate corporation and sales to another. Perhaps this was a mechanism to enforce transparent cash accounting. Alternatively, it might be a structure to remove cash from GAZ ahead of creditors. In some other Russian industries the purchasing company would mark up supplies on their way to the manufacturing company, which the sales company would buy from the manufacturing company at an artificially low price before adding another markup for sale to distributors. In this way profits could be harvested from both purchases and sales while the core manufacturer was operated at a loss in order to bleed any cash reserves.

Yet is seems unlikely that there was cash to bleed, although GAZ finances remain opaque. Why would SibAl aquire an ailing "rust belt" giant unless bright young managers believed that they could transform the company into a profitable producer of competitive vehicles? The prevailing view of Western analysts is that, following the ascension of President Putin, the smartest of the oligarchs realized that to further expand their wealth and power they must now manage successfully the industries they acquire. In general, SibAl appears to be on this course. Shortly after the GAZ acquisition, Deripaska wrote to the *Wall Street Journal:* "In the past two years my colleagues and I have created a company that is more transparent and accountable. We have made a clean break with the disreputable practices of the past by re-investing revenue—diverted offshore by our predecessors—back into Russia."[3]

Unlike a "Third World" country, Russia is a modern society with a highly educated citizenry, sophisticated scientific and technological institutions, well-developed rail and electrical infrastructures, nuclear and space capabilities, and vast reserves of the natural resources most in demand by the world economy. It has a rich culture, a deep spiritual tradition, and a population that has proved resilient in the face of adversity.

Standing in front of the GAZ Model A sedan, Richard Austin addressed the seventieth-anniversary celebration of the automobile factory. Also on the stage are GAZ president Nikolai Pugin and general director Demitry Strezhnev (seated on the left) and interpreter Alexander Sayanov (standing).

Russia lacks democratic traditions. Capital flight continues to deplete investment resources. Russia has limited experience in the world's dominant market economy. When Russians brought Communist rule to an end, American politicians, bankers, and businessmen were too eager to tell Russia how to leap toward capitalism. Much of this advice turned out poorly. It was also cheap. America was not forthcoming with substantial aid and investment in Russia following the Cold War, in comparison to what it provided Western Europe and Japan following World War II. Effectively assisting an industrious and democratic Russia may take far more investment than has yet been contemplated.

Even so, there are many cooperative ventures. Since 1999 the GAZ Museum of History and the Crawford Auto-Aviation Museum in Cleveland have been developing plans for an international exhibition on the history of Russo-American cooperation at GAZ. The new GAZ management, understanding that a noble history might support morale during a period of transition and uncertainty, scheduled for January 2002 an elaborate celebration for the seventieth anniversary of the opening of the automobile factory. I was invited to the celebration and to deliver an address. In attendance were company officials, "heroes of labor," and representatives of government and industry as well as foreign delegates from Fiat, Haden, Ford, and Austin. The evening's festivities included brief speeches by company managers and government officials as well as an American cowboy-style song-and-dance number performed by a troupe from Nizhny Novgorod.

In my remarks I spoke of the need for international cooperation:

How do we speak to one another, and listen to each other, across barriers of language, barriers of culture, barriers of history? This was not easy in 1930 and it is not easy today. Yet the secret of working together can be found in the contract which, in 1929, the Austin Company signed with the State Bureau for Building the Automobile Plant, "Autostroy." The contract said this: "If there shall arise any controversy or difficulty the parties hereto shall settle them by mutual efforts, in a friendly way."

This great factory and this city were built by people from several nations who were willing to risk the unknown and to work together for a better future. When difficulties arose, they kept their promise to "settle them by mutual efforts, in a friendly way."

Earlier in the talk my voice cracked when sharing the emotion that I feel in Nizhny Novgorod.

My father helped to supervise erection of the "Worker's City." Indeed, here stand more buildings that were touched by my father's hands every day than at any other site in the world. When I walk among those buildings I feel my father's presence.

This was Allan Austin's favorite image from his work in Nizhny Novgorod: the unfinished stairwell for the first communal housing unit erected in 1930. Seventy years later this sturdy building houses GAZ "veterans." Allan favored clean lines, functional shapes, and simple decoration reflecting materials and workmanship. The Austin Company would become America's leading practioner of such "Thirties Modern" architecture. *Allan Austin Construction Album*

NOTES

CHAPTER 2

1. Allan Nevins and Frank Ernest Hill, *Ford: Expansion and Challenge, 1915–1933* (New York: Arno Press, 1976), 2:667.
2. Kurt S. Schultz, "Building the 'Soviet Detroit': The Construction of the Nizhnii-Novgorod Automobile Factory, 1927–1932," *Slavic Review* 49 (Summer 1990): 201.
3. Quoted in Mira Wilkins and Frank Ernest Hill, *American Business Abroad: Ford on Six Continents* (Detroit: Wayne State University Press, 1964), 226.
4. Quoted in Frederick A. Van Fleet, "Building a Ford Factory in Russia," *The Review of Reviews* (January 1931).
5. Boris M. Shpotov, "Documents in the Russian State Archives of the Economy, Moscow, relevant to the joint project Austin-GAZ-Ford," 1999, no. 3, abstract and translation prepared for the Western Reserve Historical Society.
6. Quoted in Van Fleet, "Building a Ford Factory in Russia."
7. Ibid.
8. Shpotov, "Documents," nos. 8, 9.

CHAPTER 3

1. "Agreement between 'Autostroy' and The Austin Company," August 23, 1929, p. 14, article 35 ("English Agreement Original"), The Austin Company Archives.
2. Martin Greif, *The New Industrial Landscape: The Story of The Austin Company* (Clinton, N.J.: Main Street Press, 1978), 99.
3. "Agreement," p. 7, article 17.
4. Robert Scoon, "Those Communist Model A's," *The Restorer*, vol. 14 (March–April 1970), 13.
5. Harold Evans, *The American Century* (New York: Alfred A. Knopf, 1998), 280.
6. Wilkins and Hill, *American Business Abroad*, 221.

7. Schultz, "Building the 'Soviet Detroit,'" 206. His quotation is from *Za industrial-izatsiiu* [*For Industrialization*], September 14, 1930.

8. Shpotov, "Documents," nos. 15–18. The newspaper articles on February 22, March 29, and April 13, 1930.

9. Wilkins and Hill, *American Business Abroad,* 221, 222.

10. Memorandum, May 26, 1930, Nizhny Novgorod Regional Archives.

11. Memorandum, May 26, 1930, Nizhny Novgorod Regional Archives.

CHAPTER 4

1. K. Byunting, report covering April 17–23, 1930, trans. Galina Molvena, Nizhny Novgorod Regional Archives.

2. Nizhny Novgorod Regional Archives.

3. Figes, *A People's Tragedy,* 616–18.

4. Sidney Harcave, *Russia: A History* (Chicago: J. B. Lippincott, 1953), 551.

CHAPTER 5

1. Allan's reference is to Ralph Waldo Emerson's famous poem celebrating the opening battle of the American Revolution on April 19, 1775, near the villages of Lexington and Concord, Massachusetts.

   By the rude bridge that arched the flood,
   Their Flag to April's breeze unfurled,
   Here once the embattled farmers stood,
   And fired the shot heard round the world.

2. V. Lavrov , "Socialist Cities," *Moscow Construction* no. 4 (1930), trans. Galina Molvena.

3. Ibid.

4. Charles W. Wolfe to Autostroy, Moscow, May 11, 1930, Nizhny Novgorod Regional Archives.

5. Quoted in James H. Billington, *The Icon and the Axe* (New York: Vintage Books, 1970), 522, 523.

CHAPTER 6

1. Leslie Candor Farquhar, "Model A Fords and the USSR," unpublished typescript, p. 138, Western Reserve Historical Society.

CHAPTER 7

1. Boris Agapov, "Off the Road," *Za industrializatsiia* [*For Industrialization*], August 2, 1930. I rely on a translation in the The Austin Company Archives, with some corrections and additions supplied by Boris Shpotov, who examined the original text.

2. H. F. Miter, memo, "Payment of Monthy Fee," to Autostroy, Nizhny Novgorod, June 8, 1930, Nizhny Novgorod Regional Archives.
3. *Cleveland Press,* November 24, 1930, The Austin Company Archives.
4. Shpotov, "Documents," no. 19.
5. Russian State Archives of the Economy, Moscow, reprinted in Shpotov, "Documents," no. 21.
6. Shpotov, "Documents," no. 22.
7. Ibid., no. 23.; "Austin Original, Second Supplemental Agreement between Autostroy and Concern, July 18, 1930, G. A. Bryant Jr.," English Text in Austin Company Archives.
8. Schultz, "Building the 'Soviet Detroit,'" 207.
9. Clipping with date and name of newspaper, other than "Cleveland," removed, The Austin Company Archives.

CHAPTER 8

1. July 30, 1930, Nizhny Novgorod Regional Archives.
2. The original of Harry Miter's letter is bound with the letters from Allan Austin.
3. H. R. Knickerbocker, *New York Evening Post,* November 19, 1930. His dispatch from Nizhny Novgorod is filled with exaggerations and inaccuracies.

CHAPTER 10

1. Shpotov, "Documents," no. 37.
2. Ibid., no. 38.
3. Ibid., no. 39.
4. Mimeographed text of Miter's Christmas cable and original of his letter, January 17, 1931, The Austin Company archives.

CHAPTER 11

1. Nizhny Novgorod Regional Archives
2. Nizhny Novgorod Regional Archives
3. Nizhny Novgorod Regional Archives
4. Nizhny Novgorod Regional Archives
5. Milly Bennett, "Perplexing Problems of the Twenty U.S. Engineers at Nizhni Novgorod" *(Long Beach, California) Press Telegram,* August 23, 1931, and *(New Bedford, California) Times,* September 7, 1931. It was also published in the *San Francisco News* and later in three eastern U.S. newspapers (The Austin Company Archives).
6. Farquhar, "Model A Fords and the USSR," 174.

CHAPTER 12

1. Figes, *A People's Tragedy,* 749.
2. *Cleveland Plain Dealer,* November 21, 1930.

3. Figes, *A People's Tragedy,* 68–69.

4. Ibid., 116–17.

5. Ibid., 67, 745.

CHAPTER 13   1. Quotations translated from Boris Agapov in *Za industrializatsiia* [*For Industrialization*], January 7, October 12, August 23, 1931, in Schultz, "Building the 'Soviet Detroit,'" 211.

2. Bennett, "Perplexing Problems."

3. Boris Agapov, "Off the Road."

4. A. Kolchin, "Lack of Housing Hampers the Recruitment of Workers," trans. Boris Shpotov, *Trud* [*Labor*], October 17, 1931, 287.

CHAPTER 14   1. Nizhny Novgorod Regional Archives.

2. Schultz, "Building the 'Soviet Detroit,'" 208.

3. Initial contract, August 23, 1929 (see chap. 3, above); and "Second Supplemental Agreement," July 18, 1930 (see chap. 7, above).

4. Nizhny Novgorod Regional Archives.

5. Letter in George Bryant Papers, held by his grandson, Lawrence R. Myers, photocopies in Western Reserve Historical Society.

6. Walter Duranty, apparently writing in the *New York Times,* quoted by Farquhar, "Model A Fords and the USSR,"106

7. Bennett, "Perplexing Problems."

8. Shpotov, "Documents," no. 85.

9. Philip K. Davis, "The Building of Molotov," *Journal,* April 1932 (a publication of the Worchester Polytechnic Institute).

10. Schultz, "Building the 'Soviet Detroit,'" 207, 209.

11. *Za industrializatsiia* [*For Industrialization*], September 24, 1931, 264.

12. Interview with Martin Greif, August 4, 1976, The Austin Company Archives.

CHAPTER 15   1. Schultz, "Building the 'Soviet Detroit,'" 210.

2. Walter Duranty, "Mass Output Fails," *New York Times,* April 4, 1932.

3. This and subsequent Reuther quotes are in Frank Cormier and William J. Eaton, *Reuther* (Upper Saddle River, N.J.: Prentice Hall, 1970), 30–44.

4. H. F. Miter, postcard to Mr. and Mrs. Phil Davis, July 30, 1939, The Austin Company Archives.

5. Farquhar, "Model A Fords and the USSR," 181.

6. As transcribed from Alexander Sayanov's translation of Vlasov's remarks, videotape of press conference, September 23, 1999, Crawford Museum; Farquhar, "Model A Fords and the USSR," 213.

CHAPTER 16

1. Alexander Kansky, "Report on Russian Auto Industry," St. Petersburg: U.S. Foreign Commercial Service and U.S. Department of State, September 2000, <www.bisnis.doc.gov/nis/:>, para. 2.
2. *Newsweek*, International Edition, July 8, 2002, <http//stacks.msnbc.com/news/774280.asp?cp1>.
3. *Wall Street Journal Europe*, March 13, 2001.
4. "Shady Changes in Russian Business," DRUM Resources Newsletter, February 26, 2002, <DR24@drumresources.com>.

BIBLIOGRAPHY

Allan Austin's and Margretta Austin's letters and photographs have been deposited with the Austin Family Papers at the Western Reserve Historical Society. The originals of other photographs will be found at the GAZ Museum of History or at The Austin Company, as indicated in the text and notes. Original manuscript materials may be found at these locations and also at the Nizhny Novgorod State Archive and at the Russian State Archives of the Economy, Moscow.

Copies of nearly every item used in the preparation of this book have been deposited both at the Western Reserve Historical Society and at the GAZ Museum of History. Researchers in both Russia and the United States may have convenient access to them.

REPOSITORIES

The Austin Company, Mayfield Heights, Ohio
GAZ Museum of History, Nizhny Novgorod, Russia
Nizhny Novgorod State Archives, Nizhny Novgorod, Russia.
Russian State Archives of the Economy, Moscow
Walter P. Reuther Library, Wayne State University, Detroit, Michigan
    The Archives of Walter and Victor Reuther
Western Reserve Historical Society, Cleveland, Ohio
    The Austin Family Papers
    Austin/GAZ/Ford Papers

PUBLISHED SOURCES

Agapov, Boris. "Off the Road." *Za industrializatsiia* [For Industrialization], August 2, 1930.
Austin, Allan S. "Communism Builds Its City of Utopia." *New York Times Magazine*, August 9, 1931.

Billington, James. *The Icon and the Axe*. New York: Vintage Books, 1970.

Cormier, Frank, and Eaton, William J. *Reuther*. Upper Saddle River, N.J.: Prentice Hall, 1970.

Evans, Harold. *The American Century*. New York: Alfred A. Knopf, 1998.

Figes, Orlando. *A People's Tragedy: The Russian Revolution, 1891–1924*. New York: Penguin Books, 1998.

Lavrov, V. "Socialist Cities." *Moscow Construction* no. 4 (1930).

Greif, Martin. *The New Industrial Landscape: The Story of The Austin Company*. Clifton, N.J.: Main Street Press, 1978.

Harcave, Sidney. *Russia: A History*. Chicago: J. B. Lippincott, 1953.

Kansky, Alexander. "Report on Russian Auto Industry." St. Petersburg: U.S. Foreign Commercial Service and U.S. Department of State, 2000.

Nevins, Allan, and Hill, Frank Ernest. *Ford: Expansion and Challenge, 1915–1933*. New York: Arno Press, 1976.

Schoon, Robert. "Those Communist Model A's." *The Restorer* 14 (March–April 1970).

Schultz, Kurt S. "Building the 'Soviet Detroit': The Construction of the Nizhnii-Novgorod Automobile Factory, 1927–1932." *Slavic Review* 49 (Summer 1990).

Van Fleet, Frederick A. "Building a Ford Factory in Russia." *The Review of Reviews*, January 1931.

Wilkins, Mira, and Hill, Frank Ernest. *American Business Abroad: Ford on Six Continents*. Detroit: Wayne State University Press, 1964.

UNPUBLISHED SOURCES

Farquhar, Leslie Candor. "Model A Fords and the USSR." 1990.

Kugel, Barbara M. "The Export of American Technology to the Soviet Union, 1918–1933." Ph.D. diss., Wayne State University, 1956.

BUILDING UTOPIA

was designed and composed by Christine Brooks;

printed by Sheridan Books of Ann Arbor, Michigan;

and published by

THE KENT STATE UNIVERSITY PRESS

Kent, Ohio 44242